Fly Fishing

A Woman's Guide for Beginners

A comprehensive description of the essential gear. Casting techniques and a therapeutic look at the mental & physical benefits of the great outdoors.

P. Estes

DORRANCE
PUBLISHING CO
EST. 1920
PITTSBURGH, PENNSYLVANIA 15238

Dorrance Publishing Co
585 Alpha Drive
Pittsburgh, PA 15238
Visit our website at www.dorrancebookstore.com

ISBN: 979-8-88812-421-5
eISBN: 979-8-88812-921-0

Table of Contents

Introduction

I wouldn't describe myself as an athlete, but the shared love of two of the most important figures in my life, my father and grandfather, inspired me to give fly fishing a chance. So I joined them for their fishing trip one summer during my childhood. The very first time I stepped into the water, I lost my balance and fell in, butt first, into the stream. I tried not to make a big deal of it as I was optimistic that I would adapt to my "new" situation in no time.

As I attempted to go further into the water, my insecurities kept shouting, "You won't be any good. YOU WON'T BE ANY GOOD!" A small part of me fell for the voice and I paused initially because I thought "I won't be any good." I was too afraid of failure to savor the thrill of the experience and just have fun like my dad and grandpa. However, something about their happiness encouraged me to go further into the water and join them. As I took those wobbly steps toward them, despite the voice of self-doubt still ringing in my head, I knew I was taking the first steps toward a lifelong journey of the love for fly fishing. To date, I do not regret taking those steps.

Have you ever wondered whether dry fly fishing or wet fly fishing or both are a good fit for you? Do you need help selecting the basic gear that will make you effective in your fly fishing journey? Do you know how to pair the reel with the fly rod? Are you asking yourself what type of line, tippet and leader completes the fly rod? Are you concerned about how to get the sweetest deals for your money when purchasing fly fishing gear? Could you use help learning how to cast a fly rod?

If your answers to these questions were "yes," worry no more because this guide has you covered. This book provides detailed information about the necessary equipment to fly fish. It also gives the reader instructions for assembling the rod/reel/line/tippet and leader, as well as casting in the proper way. More importantly, you will learn about the mental and physical benefits of fly fishing and being outdoors.

Imagine the thrill attached to increasing your catch because you have mastered the technique of fly casting. Also, think about how your effectiveness on the water can double, even triple because you have selected the right fly fishing gear and are knowledgeable about pairing them properly. Do you know the outdoors can do wonders for your relationships? Also, know that you are well on your way to meeting your fitness goals just by engaging in fly fishing, which is a low impact workout. Reading this book is your first step toward these exciting new prospects.

The author, Patricia Estes, has been fly fishing with her father and grandfather on the American River in Northern California since she was eight years old. They spent a lot of time together fishing along the river and they grew to love the great outdoors. Although they are both gone, Patricia still fly fishes on the river and derives great joy from it.

She developed a strong bond with these key figures in her life and she intends to share these feelings of peace, as well as her passion and her enthusiasm for fly fishing with the readers. This book was written because there are few instructional books on the subject meant to motivate women toward fly fishing. The author has extensive knowledge about the sport and guarantees that a lot of the readers' questions will be answered as they dive deeper into the pages.

Are you ready to take a step? Keep reading.

What Is Fly Fishing?

Before diving into this guide, you might be asking yourself, what is fly fishing? First, let me note that 6.1 million people in the US fly fish. Fly fishing is considered one of the finest forms of angling (fishing), primarily due to the beautiful motion of fly casting, as evidenced in the movie *A River Runs Through It*. The sport is a fishing technique that uses a setup that differentiates from spin or bait fishing in that you use a "pole" in lieu of a fishing rod, the line is weighted and the casting is done in a continuous manner instead of casting and then leaving the rod until the fish bite. The idea is to trick the fish into believing that the fly is an actual insect so that they will "bite" the bait. There are a variety of flies that are used to catch fish. They range from dry flies that represent an actual copy of real flies on the surface of the water; to nymphs that are used underwater and finally streamers that often emulate small baitfish or other organisms that attract fish. Flies are used in rivers, creeks, streams, and ponds. They are also used when fishing in the ocean (saltwater fishing). In saltwater, they are used along the coastal "flats" to attract fish. The concerns with climate change and the protection of species have led to many people in different parts of the world engaging in fly fishing as a "catch-and-release" type of sport fishing, so that all fish caught are returned unharmed back to their habitat. Fly fishing offers mental, physical, social, and psychological benefits to those who practice it. Fly fishing is scientifically proven to calm our nerves. It is also useful for relaxation purposes. Additionally, it has been shown to provide a full body workout and help with depression while providing a new perspective on life.

At first, fly fishing may seem like a daunting sport. When you think about it, images of rushing water are conjured in your mind's eye and you may feel a little bit intimidated especially if you are uncomfortable around bodies of water. However, anyone at all can learn fly fishing. By learning some initial steps and understanding the basics, you will be well on your way to enjoying fly fishing.

Chapter 1: Mental and Physical Benefits of Fly Fishing

In today's hectic world of Covid-19, with higher prices for just about everything, and the battle for climate change, this healthy hobby is the gateway you need to the state of mind you desire. Whether you are dealing with stress, depression, the inability to sleep at night, lack of exercise, or the inability to relax completely, fly fishing is therapeutic while also providing a clearer perspective.

Mental Benefits of Fly Fishing

Fly Fishing Is an Avenue for Relaxation

The back and forth movement of the rod, line, and fly is a well-needed distraction to take your mind off your normal train of thought. Your attention is directed toward the fly and casting it in the direction that you intend, which allows you to focus on the positive while removing negative thought patterns. Like meditation, this intense concentration can move you from the negative, directly into the positive. Relaxation is instilled by the sound of rushing water soothing the mind and the concentration of placing the fly exactly where it is intended to go. The fluidity of the casting (line) is a somewhat hypnotic element as the concentration is so intense. Although not as popular as yoga, exercise or other well-known sports, fly fishing is a great way to reduce the stress factors in our lives.

Fly Fishing Reduces Stress

The following statistics from a Med Alert Help, 2022 study emphasize the stress we find ourselves in.

- Med Alert Help reports that the lowest stress levels are recorded in adults older than 72.
- The same website reports that 80% of millennials are stressed about money, as millennials' stress statistics show.
- Med Alert Help also claims that teenagers report a stress level of 5.8 out of 10 during the school year.
- One in five college students has thought about suicide.
- China has seen the highest rise in workplace stress.
- 83% of Americans are worried about the future of the nation.

- Nearly 25% of people report feeling extreme stress during the holidays.
- 45% of college students seek counseling due to stress.
- Around 70% of students are often or always stressed about schoolwork.
- Only 14% of US citizens exercise regularly to handle stress.

According to the study conducted on stress, concern about finances was the cause of stress for 67% of respondents, followed closely by work issues for 65% of the volunteers.. Other studies report that adults were more prone to consider personal health issues, the economy, duties toward loved ones, and the health condition of these significant figures as stressful. Those who look up to other people for care and support, such as minors and the aged, or those who are marginalized in society due to their skin color, their sex, and literacy, among others, are more likely to develop stress-related health problems. Similar factors may include physical weakness, heightened feelings of rage and insecurity, as well as the inability to trust other people. Experts have stated that some levels of stress are needed for all living things because it is their natural way of responding to changes in their environment, and they even mention that the good or bad things that happen to us account for the stress generated in our lives. Professionals believe that a greater proportion of modern diseases are stress-related.

The signs that you are stressed can manifest both physically and psychologically. Stress-related physical illnesses, such as irritable bowel syndrome (IBS) or irritable bowel disease (IBD), heart attacks, arthritis, and chronic headaches, result from long-term overstimulation of a part of the nervous system that regulates the heart rate, blood pressure, and digestive system (Med Alert Help, 2022). The emotional illnesses attached to stress are a result of poor methods of handling life problems, some of which can include the loss of a loved one, being involved in an accident, and not being able to cater to yourself and your dependents financially, among many other issues.

Everywhere people are constantly saying how tired and stressed they are. Everyone needs to unwind from the stress that comes with life. In the war against stress in our lives, fly fishing offers one of the most promising positive effects of being in the great outdoors. Significant exposure to the outdoors has also been linked to the reduction of "mental fatigue". The rivers, trees, and sky are relaxing for the mind. Improving your mental health is a huge step in reducing stress. The soothing sound of a rushing stream as it works against the rocks or the lapping waves as they hit the side of your boat promotes relaxation.

Fly Fishing Provides a Cure for Depression
Anxiety and depression are fast blowing out of proportion to become global pandemics in our modern world. More people are victims of mental illness today than at any other time in history. Millions of people are dealing with some sort of mental health problem in the US alone. With the numbers increasing by the day, it is not difficult to figure out why an

increasing number of people are gravitating toward practices to manage their mental health. More people are engaging in yoga and deep forms of meditation because of the health benefits attached to them. In a bid to maintain their mental well-being, a greater section of people are looking for diverse forms of sporting activities that allow them to have fun and at the same time have benefits for their psychological health. A lot of individuals in society are still unaware of the benefits of fly fishing as far as curing anxiety and depression is concerned. Even some who engage in the sport do not fully appreciate the essence of this exercise to their psychological well-being. The flowing water and fresh air can have an almost instantaneous effect on your mood and prevent feelings of anxiety, fatigue, and depression. The time you spend fly fishing is therapeutic in the sense that it produces fewer levels of activity in the brain's prefrontal cortex. This makes it much easier to avoid recycling negative thoughts and to break out of negative feelings and emotions. This eventually reduces your stress levels. A high level of concentration, coupled with the rhythmic movement of casting have calming effects on anyone who participates in the sport. Fly fishing is a great outdoor activity and an efficient form of therapy. The natural setting is meditation-friendly. Focusing on the bait and the catch allows you to concentrate on the task at hand and take your mind off your problems.

Fly Fishing Provides an Avenue for Networking

We are social creatures, we need to connect with others. Fly fishing can help reinforce an old friendship or make new ones. Acquaintances formed in the great outdoors, while fishing, could be the start of a budding new friendship that may remain with you for life.

Loneliness is one cause of anxiety and depression. This can spiral into a negative web where drugs and alcohol could get involved if not controlled. Meeting people outside of your circle can seem daunting, but fly fishing is a great way to network with like-minded souls. Because of the increasing demand placed on our time, and the constant busyness in our lives, more people are feeling lonelier today than at any other time in human history. Chronic loneliness is a major cause of a lot of mental health problems. However, everyone can make time for the things that have meaning for them. So, you can make time to initiate and maintain rewarding connections by bonding with your family and loved ones when you go fly fishing. Making plans to go fly fishing with your friends and family once in a while is an advisable line of action. Also, joining a fishing club to spend time and network with like-minded anglers in the great outdoors is a great alternative. Fly fishing strengthens your bonds and makes you a part of a unique community. By exchanging your knowledge and life experiences, you connect with people and develop mutual trust and respect for each other. Your highs and lows shared during your fly fishing journey build empathy and are a means of forging solid friendships with people who eventually become like family. It is also a great way to make memories that remain with you for life.

Joining other people when fly fishing adds a whole new element of fun to the experience. Whether with a relative, a lover, or a longtime friend, you will realize that the thrill of the experience is multiplied when shared with another person. My entire family from my grandfather and grandmother, dad, and mom, uncles, and cousins all share a love of the outdoors. Their passions are fishing of all kinds, hunting, and camping. We spent every summer camping at Union Valley Reservoir in El Dorado County, about 20 miles from Placerville. It was the BEST time of my life because my whole family was together for a week, right down to grandma doing all the cooking over an open fire; fresh trout, sliced potatoes, pork and beans...my mouth is watering just thinking about it. After dinner, listening to stories, family histories, fishing and hunting trips told by various members of the family. Recounting funny times and sad times. My dad had a million of them.

Fly Fishing Boosts Your Brain Power

You need to constantly practice to become a proficient angler. You also need to be patient to learn the skill of casting into the right places where fish are more likely to be found. Moreover, you need to utilize a good deal of brain power to become a master of fly fishing techniques. It takes time to research and learn how to fly fish, all of which are activities that work certain parts of the brain. The focused concentration and attention to detail required during fly fishing help to strengthen the potential of your brain. It allows you to clear your head and improves your thinking capacity. The fresh outdoor air can have major advantages for your short-term memory. Studies have shown that even a little time spent outdoors can have profound effects on your capacity to recall information and boost your short-term memory by as much as 20%. The trees, moving waters, and the clean air all have healing properties that rejuvenate not only the body but also the mind. A study has shown that one can even envigorate one's mental state, and reduce mental fatigue just by staring at pictures of nature and the outdoors. Imagine the boost one gains by visiting the outdoors and nature in person. Go out and explore everything that nature has to offer. Spending time fly fishing clears the mind and improves your thinking capacity. A clearer mind also paves the way for creativity. Some successful novelists, scriptwriters, and poets have advocated the wonders that the outdoors have had on their creative powers.

Fly Fishing Gives You Perspective

Fly fishing offers you the opportunity to acquire a new perspective on the happenings in your daily life. It ignites your creative powers which prepares you to find strategic ways to cope with the challenges that come with life.

Fly Fishing Boosts Your Self-Esteem

When you decide to take courses on fly fishing and study all the resources to help you perfect your craft, you position yourself for success in this field. When you eventually master the skill of casting and catching fish with your fly rod, you get an improved sense of self-worth. You set and shatter your records which is a big drive to propel you toward more daring exploits.

Fly Fishing Increases Feelings of Happiness and Excitement

The thrill of missing a fish with your fly rod and then eventually catching one excites the spirits. It is also a relief to leave your normal routine and try something that you do not usually do. The proximity to nature and the chance to imbibe fresh air is a booster for both your physical and mental faculties. Fly fishing also prevents feelings of tiredness and depression by leveling your melatonin levels. It also allows you to take a break from your normal activities and unwind accordingly.

Fly Fishing Is Therapeutic

A lot of people consider fly fishing as their favorite and most relaxing pastime, and for good reason. Fly fishing offers the individual the chance to unwind. It also offers proximity to nature, and the chance to catch fish either for food or just for fun. But more than this, fly fishing improves the individual's mental state. It is a healthy exercise to engage in. The focused effort it entails engages both the mind and the body to finally achieve the desired effect. Getting outside can help you to break out of a cycle of negative thoughts. So fly fishing is a good exercise to participate in if you are looking to de-stress and get out of your head. It is also a great way to reconnect with nature. Also, you feel a rush of excitement and adrenaline when you make a catch because these hormones and feelings are connected with achievement—no wonder this type of sport is recommended for survivors of war and those dealing with trauma.

Fly fishing has often been described as calming, relaxing, and peaceful. It provides a Zen feeling, while also exhibiting art. The "Art" of fly fishing is pursuing the perfect cast, the perfect drift, the perfect presentation.

Fly Fishing Improves Focus and Patience

Since the advent and improvement of modern technology people have become more attached to their gadgets. They are constantly bombarded with notifications, which eventually dull their concentration and shorten their attention span. This makes it significantly harder for people to focus on the things that truly matter. Because of the demand of modern apps and social media, time spent in the outdoors is appreciated by both body and mind since it provides a disconnect from technology, and those other things that are constantly placing a demand on our time. Fly fishing has a calming and meditative effect on your brain. This helps to boost your concentration.

Letting Go and Non-Attachment

You can decide to pay attention to your breath as you hold the fly rod, coordinating your inhale and exhale with the movement of the cast, calming your mind and body. Furthermore, you can fix your eyes on anything floating on the surface of the water as it floats along. Both strategies provide an immediate form of relief and relax your whole body.

Physical Benefits of Fly Fishing

Fly Fishing Lowers Your Cortisol Level

People who engage in fly fishing as a pastime experience lower cortisol (stress hormone) levels. Their stress levels are reduced and they have improved sleep. Anglers are also less likely to exhibit Post Traumatic Stress Disorder (PTSD) symptoms and experience lower levels of depression and anxiety.

Fly Fishing Offers a Full Body Workout

Fly Fisher Pro reports that you burn an average of 234 calories per hour when fly fishing. This is almost the same number of calories you burn when you run on a treadmill. The same website further reports that a few hours of fly fishing can result in the individual burning up 700-1600 calories. Rowing, climbing, and casting also engage the muscles in your arms. Again, reeling in fish works the same kinds of muscles, especially if they play against you. You exercise unconsciously when you engage in fly fishing. Spending time in the water works your body and your mind, although these may not be as intense as the kinds of workouts associated with the gym, like resistance training and aerobic exercises. However, you work your shoulders, core, arms, back muscles, and legs when you are fly fishing without the boredom of the gym.

If you are not cut out for the grueling exercise routine which is normally done in the gym, fly fishing is a great alternative. The probabilities of sustaining injuries while engaging in this sport are less because it is low impact. Also, fly fishing can be done at any time of the day. The kind of pollution associated with the city can be detrimental to your health, so the fresh air and uniqueness of the outdoors are needed by the body as it helps to detoxify your lungs as well as your entire body. This is because the air outdoors, away from crowds, is less polluted compared to city air. When fly fishing, the rushing stream produces negative ions which have been shown to strengthen the immune system. These types of ions are also known to increase metabolism and regulate sleep patterns, as well as having healing effects on your overall being. The cleaner air outdoors is good for your health. Fly fishing at the beginning of the day exposes you to the morning sun which is rich in vitamin D. This vitamin is healthy and aids in the absorption of calcium. Prolonged stays in the outdoors can also improve feelings of wellness.

Fly fishing is a great divergence from the sedentary routine of many office workers. It is also an advisable sport for anyone who remains stationary for the better part of the day. If intense workouts or jogging are activities that you particularly despise, fly fishing offers just the right amount of physical movement to engage your muscles without stretching them to their limits. Fly fishing requires movement, sometimes for several hours at a time. This movement supports blood flow and adequate circulation which is useful for preventing stiffness. Casting and reeling are useful for working your upper body. These movements engage your arm muscles and shoulders with the least possible strain on your wrists. This works best when you are casting correctly and practicing good form. Also, when you are trying to maintain your stance in a moving stream when fishing, you engage your back muscles, legs, and core. Fly fishing is for people of all ages. Seniors looking to engage in less intense forms of workout can consider fly fishing. The exercise is less demanding compared to those done in the gym and you get to choose the extent of your movement on the fishing trip. You can choose your fly fishing expeditions to accommodate whether you want to hike for a few miles to get to a stream or river while at other times you could decide to fish where you only have to walk a few yards from where you park.

Fly Fishing Has Healing Properties

Fly fishing has great healing properties for physical injuries and ailments. Being outdoors is known to reduce inflammation. Inflammation is the body's innate mechanism for fighting against injury, contaminants and infection. However, in some instances, it goes beyond a useful reaction and blows out of proportion to become harmful swelling as well as autoimmune issues. The natural environment is known to reduce unnecessary swelling in individuals who engage in outdoor sports. Fly fishing, for example, helps to heal an inflamed part of the body just by standing in a cool stream or river. Fly fishing is also known to improve eyesight. A connection has been found between long periods of exposure to nature and the reduced risk of developing nearsightedness in children. That is a great reason to get your entire family away from their phones and televisions and out into nature.

The Nine Best Locations For Fly Fishing In The United States

Depending where you live, or if you'd like to travel to enjoy the outdoors, here are my favorite best travel destinations within the US. First, we have California. The remaining eight states are; Montana (big sky country), West Virginia, Alaska, Florida, Colorado, Wyoming, Pennsylvania and North Carolina.

California

We begin with California as this is the author's home state and an area that is very well-known for its great rivers. This location is home to the Yuba River, the Sacramento River, the Yosemite National Park, and the Owens River, all of which are great places for fly fishing.

Montana

Montana is home to Rock Creek, which contains a wide variety of fish. Some of the available options are different species of trout. The scenery is also easy on the eye.

West Virginia

The famous Gauley River is situated in West Virginia. The New River, Gorge National River, and Bluestone National Scenic River are other great locations for fly fishing. There are a rich variety of fish located in each of these rivers. The natural beauty of these outdoor locations is also one of a kind.

Alaska

There are so many rivers in Bristol Bay, Alaska. The Nushagak River and Togiak River are just a few. These waters boast a great deal of wild sockeye salmon, rainbow trout and so many other varieties of fish.

Colorado

Colorado is home to the famous Colorado River as well as the Blue River. Despite the intense sun in this state, a lot of anglers enjoy fishing there.

Florida

Florida is known for saltwater fly fishing. The Florida Keys, for instance, are rich in various species of fish including tarpon and bonefish.

Wyoming

The Snake River is found in Wyoming. It boasts some of the largest fish and is a choice location for many anglers.

Pennsylvania

Some of the most well-known limestone streams, springs, and creeks are found in Pennsylvania. Anglers have been fishing at these spots for generations.

North Carolina

This state hosts a stretch of water that is home to different species of fish, especially trout. Fly fishers have been using this spot for generations and it is a great place to visit.

Chapter 2: The Six Best Fly Fishing Vests and the Reasons Why

In order to engage in this wonderful sport you will need some gear. Let's start with some basics. Fly fishing vests are necessary attire that makes the work of the angler much easier. Their sole purpose is for the safekeeping of fly fishing equipment. If you need access to a specific tool at a particular moment, you can quickly access it. Again, if you find it necessary to switch your tippet, you can get it quickly. It reduces the chances of finding yourself in embarrassing situations where you arrive at the stream only to realize that you have not brought your forceps along. Although a lot of people prioritize fishing vests, there is little that distinguishes the best vests from the rest. Consider them a utilitarian garment with lots of pockets and not likely to make a fashion statement. It is not essential to spend more money on vests just because they are produced by a respected brand.

Some Elements All Good Fishing Vests Must Possess

Pockets

The ideal fly fishing vest must have a number of pockets of different sizes. These vests need to be able to store a lot of fly boxes. Many anglers overdo it and have really large fishing vests that swallow them up when they wear them. Having a variety of both larger and smaller pockets allows you to keep all sizes of accessories safely and conveniently accessible.

Velcro

A lot of fly anglers love Velcro. Some even prefer these to zippers. Pockets sealed with Velcro are very easy to open and close even when wearing gloves. In addition, Velcro is very durable. Because even quality zippers wear out with time, a lot of people want their pockets to come with Velcro closures. Many people gravitate toward Velcro because it makes it easier and faster for them to access their gear for fly fishing without the hassle of zipping and unzipping their pockets anytime they want to reach for a piece of equipment. Although Velcro seals are not as secure, they are easy to use and often close on their own when your mind is elsewhere. With zipper closures, if you are feeling slightly lazy or forgetful and do not remember to close one, all your accessories may come tumbling into the water when you are still in the process of netting a fish. This has happened more times than I care to admit.

Quality Zippers

Zippers are essential, but they ought to be of satisfactory quality. A good zipper is needed for the safekeeping of accessories that are too valuable to lose. Take for example your license. Most people love zippers on pockets they do not often open. There, they store their license, keys, and sometimes their wallet. They keep these valuables in internal zipper pockets because they know they will be carrying them while in the rushing water, therefore they have to be secured somewhere that will reduce the chances of losing them. Zipper design is important. There is nothing worse than a zipper that corrodes quickly and becomes stuck easily. The zipper must also be big enough so that you can grasp it with ease, whether wearing gloves or with bare hands. They must be strong enough to survive dunking and a few silt grains between their teeth.

Clips and Attachment Points

Opt for permanently attached loops or rings where a lanyard or small carabiner can be secured. This is to prevent losing simple tools such as line clippers and forceps.

Quick drying

Anglers love a fishing vest that can dry quickly. A vest that holds moisture makes a good environment for mold growth. It also increases the odds that the metallic equipment stored within it will corrode quickly.

Color

Many anglers want fishing vests that match their surroundings. Sometimes, these colors can be pale brown fishing clothing as opposed to brighter tan ones. It is worth getting a specific shade of color if you usually go fly fishing in a particular habitat. This will allow you to better blend in with your environment. Camouflage is always an option.

Fishing Vest or Fishing Pack

This boils down to personal preference. Fishing packs come in handy if you intend to take a lot of gear with you to the location where you will be fishing. However, some people would rather wear vests. When these anglers plan to spend all day fly fishing, they usually carry a lot of items that may not fit into a fishing pack. Because of this, they just take along a small hiking pack to store their lunch, accessories, and clothing. Hiking packs are usually less expensive and are better designed. They are useful when there are simply too many items to fit inside most fly fishing packs. Alternatively, you might want to purchase a large fly fishing pack, but then there is the burden of carrying that extra weight on shorter trips. Many anglers prefer a vest and a pack because of the flexibility that combination offers. Another reason to consider a vest is because of its streamlined nature, allowing you to navigate your way around branches and through thick vegetation with less hassle.

Recommendations for Fly Fishing Vests

As you analyze the vests in this section, you will realize that many of them, which were designed by some of the most respected brands, are overdone. They either have too many pockets, zippers, and features or just possess a lot of components that might not be necessary. The purpose of a fishing vest is to make it easier to carry fishing gear from place to place. This does not imply that the designs of these vests have to be intricate. Often, it may appear as though the manufacturers are attempting to fit as many pockets and features onto a single vest. The result is a bulky mass that swallows up the one who wears it. In this section, there are some suggestions about which fishing vests are the best based on their features. Interestingly, most of them come with a lot of pockets and other extra elements. If you enjoy taking a lot of tools with you on your fly fishing expedition, then this section is one you should look at.

Simms Freestone Fishing Vest

Simms products have a lot of fans around the world. Many people trust this fly fishing brand because their vests last for a long time. It is a well-known fact among the users of Simms products that it makes some of the best fly fishing vests. The Freestone Fishing vest, for example, is a great product and also one of the most affordable vests from Simms. Another section of the population also gravitates toward the Simms Headwater Pro due to the wide range of Velcro pockets. It has a number of Hypalon tool attachment points for fastening lanyards. They reduce the chance of forgetting or losing a costly set of forceps or clippers. The vests come in a variety of natural shades, useful for those wanting to break away from the usual monotone vest colors that anglers usually wear. A few models also come in faint camouflage patterns. Overall, the Simms Freestone Fishing vest is popular among many anglers because of its quality. You can buy the product directly from Simms or from Amazon.

Patagonia Mesh Master II Vest

The Patagonia Mesh Master II is the preferable option for summer days where the environment is very sunny. Its mesh-heavy design breathes extremely well. It is manufactured with convenience at its core. It is made up of six main vertical front pockets, all with secure Velcro seals. You can easily access your equipment without wasting time with zippers. However, for the safe keeping of your tools and accessories, there are two large zipped side pockets and a lot of internal pockets. This is a great option for storing tippets (to be explained later on). The vertical layout of the vest reduces the entire bulk. Like most fly fishing vests, the Patagonia Mesh Master II is made with two tool attachment points. The back of the vest comes with two large pockets, perfectly suited for storing a light lunch and snacks. Overall, this is a very well-thought-out fly fishing vest. The downside is that the front pockets are quite deep which may require some digging to retrieve some smaller items. Being highly organized is very essential to getting the most out of the design of this vest. It is one of the more expensive fly fishing vests on the market.

Columbia Men's Henry's Fork V Vest

As a brand, this manufacturer provides a more affordable product at almost the same quality as some of the top vests in the industry. It is similar in design to the Simms Freestone, although the pockets are much larger. Although the Simms Freestone has a better quality design, the Columbia Henry's Fork is almost the same quality but is less expensive.

Gihuo Men's Fishing Vest

This vest is from one of the less popular Chinese brands. They sell a large number of their products on Amazon. The design of this vest is fairly pleasant, and it comes with a lot of pockets. Featuring several Velcro and many zippered pockets, the Gihuo vest offers a lot of space for storage. The manner in which it is constructed is unique and comfortable. It is not the heaviest of fabrics, and probably not up to the task of navigating through thick vegetation, but overall, its quality is fairly decent. It comes in a variety of forms, including fabric and mesh. The mesh version offers warm weather comfort. It comes with three attachment points for retractors or pliers. It is available in several shades of natural colors, which makes it a choice option for matching any environment. So if you are following a strict budget for buying a fishing vest, this product offers a lot of value.

Astral Ronny Life Jacket PFD

Combining a personal flotation device (PFD) and a fishing vest requires compromise. Most PFD designs prioritize security, so prepare yourself to come in contact with vests that are liberal when it comes to using bright colors. You need to keep in mind that you are more likely to frighten the fish if you appear arrayed in bright colors. The Astral Ronny Life Jacket has a lot of useful components. As a combination fishing vest and lifejacket many anglers believe it is one of the best. A fishing PFD is never going to be quite as versatile as a fishing vest designed for a single purpose, but the Astral Ronny offers a good selection of pockets and can store a good number of equipment. It is manufactured in such a way that it does not restrict arm movement. Its weight is so light that people are hardly aware that they are wearing it. Again, its design does not restrict casting in any way. Overall, it is a great fishing PFD which is a choice pick for deep wading near river mouths or fishing from a boat. Also, it is perfect for use in areas where there are concerns about footing stability.

NRS Chinook Fishing PFD

The NRS Chinook Fishing PFD is a quality product, with a wide range of pockets and attachment points. It also comes with a rod holder.

Fish Pond Upstream Tech Vest

This is the best choice for fly fishers who want it all. It is large enough with enough room for four big fly boxes. It comes with several attachment points for multiple tools. This vest comes with 14 interior and exterior pockets. In case you plan to bring an extra reel, more fly boxes, and even more spools of tippet for a fishing trip, you should consider picking this vest. Fish Pond produces some of the best fishing gear, and the Upstream Tech vest is just one of their many exceptional innovations. It is also durable. Although some anglers prefer fewer zippers and more Velcro, this vest is also a great option to consider. It is the dream come true for many and one of the best vests for any angler.

Chapter 3: Waders For Women and What to Wear Underneath

Waders are one of the most important items of gear for fly fishing for anyone. Who wants to get wet and cold when wading into a river or a lake bank? The most important thing to remember about waders, is to urinate first before putting them on (personal tip). Waders come in various styles from the full bib, waist level, or hip huggers depending on your personal preference and terrain. The clothing beneath your waders is paramount to being able to cast easily, stay cool or warm, and just being comfortable during the entire day. Boots and the right socks are a necessity as well, to deal with the mud, water, and footing. These are just personal preferences as there are all kinds available. Just be sure to pick good premium wading boots and wading socks.

Choosing the Correct Pair of Fishing Waders

Your choice of waders determines whether or not you allow mud and grime into your boots. Manufacturers have designed a variety of waders over the years and each comes with its pros and cons. The bodies of water you usually fish in and the type of fishing you engage in are key determinants of your choice of fishing waders. Some of the very popular ones on the market include hip waders, waist-high waders, and chest high waders.

Hip Waders
These are very comfortable and cost less compared to the other wading systems which will be mentioned in this section. This will be a choice option for the casual fisherman. Hip waders are water-resistant boots that, obviously, reach up to your hip area. You can consider buying them if you are someone who places little emphasis on warmth and usually fish in shallower waters.

Waist-High Waders.
These are typically waterproof pants that do not exceed the length of the waist. These waders are convenient especially on hot days because they keep you cool. Also, you can put them on without any hassle. It is the choice option for some anglers during hot seasons.

Chest High Waders

Although they can cost an arm and a leg, these are very versatile products which are very popular in the fly fishing community. Chest high waders are useful during warmer months or cold ones, and when navigating either deeper or shallower waters.

Understanding Modern Materials

Waders are usually made with waterproof materials, and in recent years, many manufacturers are designing them with materials that are lightweight because customers are more inclined toward such products. Neoprene and GORE-TEX for example last long and are popular with a lot of waders.

Neoprene

Neoprene waders are stretchy and provide warmth for the user. They are also lightweight and this is one of the reasons which accounts for their popularity. During colder seasons, many anglers rely on this type of wader. More importantly, they are affordable. Its thickness varies depending on the intended use. The thickest neoprene waders are guaranteed to produce more warmth. The downside, however, is that the thicker it is, the heavier and more inelastic it will be. Another shortfall of these types of waders is that they are less durable.

Breathable Fabrics

Water-resistant and breathable materials are dominating the fly fishing market and we will understand why in this section. These fabrics are known to block out water but serve as a great escape for bodily perspiration. Breathable waders have come to be considered something of an all-purpose product. Adding or removing layers worn underneath is an option for the user to consider if they are looking to keep their bodies at a certain temperature. Just like neoprene waders, breathable waders come in varying levels of thickness. So you are advised by manufacturers and store owners to consider the thickness of the fabric before buying a pair of breathable waders. A lot of breathable waders have more layers at the lower ends than at the chest areas because the lower portions are subjected to more stress. The material itself is heavy-duty nylon. Expensive waders are manufactured with thicker nylon whereas the less costly ones are made with paper-thin nylon that can tear easily.

A Guide to Fishing Footwear

More often than not, waders are sold alongside boots, however, nowadays, people usually buy "stockingfoot waders" first and then wading boots to wear over them separately. These waders are water-resistant, yet the boots are needed to keep your feet safe. You also have to consider the material which is used for making the sole of these boots. Some come with felt soles, rubber lug soles, as well as those which come with metal studs.

Felt Soles

Throughout the years, felt has been one of the de facto materials used for making wading boot soles because it is able to withstand slippery, wet surfaces. It is especially useful in water bodies that are mostly sandy underneath and contain great quantities of slime and algae. Nonetheless, felt has its downsides. It does not last long and has little traction when navigating paths that are full of mud. However, it is thought of as the ideal material when you want to remain stable while in the water.

Rubber Soles

Recently, many manufacturers are designing boots with Vibram rubber soles. When compared to felt, these rubber soles provide poorer traction on slippery surfaces, however, they are great products that can be used to hike and walk long distances. Typically, they last longer and can be used for different purposes. Some states prohibit the use of felt soles as a result of environmental concerns so a lot of anglers have fallen on the ones made with rubber as an alternative.

Studded Soles

Studs are basically metallic cleats that either come with your boots or are purchased separately and installed on the boots thereafter. Studs are useful for stabilizing the angler while they are in the water and for increasing the amount of traction when the soles come in contact with a slippery surface. In deeper waters with stronger currents and on wet surfaces, studded soles are great options to consider.

Buying Based on Your Fishing Style

The cost of waders varies depending on many factors, some of which include the manufacturer and the quality of the product in question. Some are as affordable as $100 and others go for as much as $800. There are so many more waders on the market now than at any other time in history so you need to be very intentional about the product you purchase. You need to take into account certain things such as whether or not the product lasts long, where you will be fishing, and the time spent in the water.

Durability

How long your waders last depend on a lot of factors, but the most important is the strength of the fabric used to design them. Some other factors are the periods dedicated to fishing and the activities performed while you are at it. When the time is spent pushing through thick bushes and other activities of the sort, you need to purchase a quality pair of waders. Although it might cost you, it is still a great investment. Meanwhile, if you do not fish as much, then you should not worry too much about how long they last. Breathable waders are known to last long, and as with anything good, they tend to be a little pricey.

Longevity

Nothing in life lasts permanently, and your wader will experience a degradation in its quality at a point in time, but how soon this happens depends on the quality of your wader and how often it is used. If you decide to make fly fishing a lifestyle, then you must be ready to invest in a brand of wader that is trusted to last long. These are usually more expensive. However, if you do not fish very often, then you could be happy with a less expensive wader.

Fishing Environment

You need to take into account the environment where you usually fish before deciding the type of wader to buy. If you usually fish in small streams and creeks, then you should consider buying a pair of hip waders. Waist-high waders are an ideal fit if you fish in meadow streams that are not too large. Go for chest waders if you usually fish in larger bodies of water. It is worth noting that chest waders are a good fit for the aforementioned three types of water. They are versatile products and are preferred by a lot of anglers for this reason. However, you have to start with waders which will not put a strain on your budget. Nonetheless, the more expensive waders are better in quality and are more durable. So you need to consider different sizes before making your final choice. Your final choice should usually depend on your environment, how often you will be fishing and the intensity of the activities you engage in. Also, think about your style of wading and your level of proficiency. All these things have to be planned beforehand to allow you to make the best possible choice when it comes to the waders.

What Should You Wear Under Waders?

Before selecting your fly fishing gear, you need to take into account the cost, weather, and items you already have. You can choose the number of layers you want to dress in but wear as many as you can so that you can either remove or add to them based on your preference and changing weather conditions. This will make it possible to avoid overheating. It is advisable to plan what you wear under your waders. You should wear a sleek base layer shirt to allow for smooth casting, a thin long-sleeved shirt on top that you can layer and take off as needed, and a nice rain jacket on top to keep out the elements

(Matechak, 2022). If you will be fishing for a long time, wading leggings and woolen socks must be worn for warmth.

Proper Clothing to Wear for Fishing

This section advises anglers on the proper clothing to wear and what not to wear since there are good and bad clothing options as far as fly fishing is concerned.

Clothing to Wear Under Waders Based on the Season

Winter and Very Cold Weather

Warmth is essential, especially during the winter. A sleek, tight base layer such as a workout Under Armor shirt is ideal as the sleekness will let your arms glide seamlessly when you cast (Matechak, 2022). Additionally, a vest can be worn to increase your bodily warmth. Hoodies can be added to these because the hood can act as a windbreak which you might need. A jacket can be a great top layer. A wading jacket is also useful, especially in cold weather. A light rain jacket is another great option to consider. Wading leggings will make great bottoms. Wearing a pair of thermal wader pants keeps your legs and feet warm when you are in cold water. Thick wool socks are also advisable options to consider. Some people prefer to wear a number of lighter socks as an alternative but this can hurt your toes and even result in blisters. Cotton socks retain water so they are usually not recommended by experts. Wool socks are moisture-wicking and hence are great for body insulation.

Spring, Summer, and Fall

It is not as important to wear layers of clothing during the summer. However, you must put on the appropriate clothing to maintain the proper body temperature when you are on the water. T-shirts, jeans, work pants, and wader pants are some of the appropriate options to consider. However, wearing shorts on the water is not advisable. Carrying a lightweight jacket also helps to protect yourself from the elements. Taking extra layers with you is also a prudent action as you are prepared for any changes in the weather. Wearing thinner socks during the summer will not have any debilitating effects.

Avoid Wearing These Under Waders

It is important to keep in mind that there is certain clothing that should not be worn beneath waders. These pieces of clothing are known to cause discomfort and even injure users. Sometimes, wearing them would cause you no harm but a lot of professionals do not recommend using them. Ankle socks for instance are one example. Full-length woolen socks are a better option. It is especially useful during colder seasons. Also, do not wear a lot of cotton fabric under your waders. Cotton does not dry quickly. Wool fabrics, on the other hand, dry quicker. Also, do not wear double layers of fleece. A fleece vest is useful apparel, however, wearing a fleece long-sleeve beneath restricts your movements and can hamper fluid casting. Some people wear sweatpants under waders. Sweatpants are usually thick so they can compress your legs when you are in the water. Furthermore, it takes a long time for them to dry. Some people wear windbreakers beneath their waders. Windbreakers are useful, however, wearing them with metal buttons is the problem. The buttons can become uncomfortably cold and imagine what will happen when they come in touch with your bare skin. You might not be as effective as you plan to be because of the discomfort. Additionally, avoid wearing sneakers with your waders. Sneakers should not be an alternative to wading boots. Wading boots can be costly, but they are worth the investment. If you cannot afford them, you can borrow some used ones from your angling pals. The reason why a lot of experts do not recommend using sneakers is that they do not provide ankle stability, which is necessary especially when you are in the water and on rocky bottoms. Wading boots, on the other hand, keep your feet safe, provide the necessary traction, and make sure that your ankles are stable in the water.

Is It Advisable To Wear Jeans Beneath Waders?

There is nothing wrong with wearing jeans under waders. They are decent pieces of apparel. However, wearing them in water will make them clutch to your legs and this might cause discomfort. Damp jeans may also not feel right against your skin. Moreover, jeans do not dry quickly. In some instances, they can remain damp for the rest of the day. So the most recommended pieces of clothing to wear under waders are wader pants or leggings although they do tend to be a bit pricey. Even work pants that are made of khaki material are a better option than jeans. They might also cling tight to your legs in water but the effect is milder on your skin. The best time to adopt jeans is in the winter.

Should Shorts Be Worn Beneath Waders?

It is not advisable to wear shorts under waders. Although shorts are comfortable, it is not a very good decision to pair them with waders. The waders cling to your legs when you are in the water. The pressure on the waders increases with the depth of your legs in the water. The materials used to make the waders can be irritating to your exposed skin. Also, wearing shorts under waders makes you feel the full intensity of the coolness of the water. In no time, a biting chill can seep in even during the summer if the water temperature is colder.

Should You Wear Socks with Waders?

It is advisable to wear socks with waders. Stockingfoot waders are water-resistant and this prevents water from seeping through them and coming in contact with your feet. Socks protect your feet too. People who do not wear socks are usually the ones who complain about getting blisters. Socks also prevent slippery feet. Thick wool socks are advisable especially in the winter. The thickness determines the kind of warmth it will give. You quickly become cold when wading in cold water. Good pants and thick socks will save you when that happens. Merino wool socks are a great option to consider. The WETSOX frictionless wader socks are a convenient option to wear under your waders. They provide warmth to your legs when you are in the river and are a quick drying material thus making them a great combination with breathable waders.

Wader Leggings

These pieces of clothing can be worn under waders throughout the year. In the hotter seasons like summer, these leggings can keep you cool and absorb sweat on your legs. They are also very comfortable to wear. In winter, you can wear more than one wader legging underneath your waders to provide warmth. Wader leggings are also recommended by many professionals. There are a variety of styles available so you can browse through them before you select the one which best suits your needs. Also, there are several pants on the market that provide warmth and you can purchase quality pairs for anything between $20-$80. Wading leggings and thermal pants are a good addition to your apparatus especially when you will be staying in the water for long periods.

Recommendations to Consider

Wading Boots

The Simms Tributary Wading Boot provides good traction, is convenient, and is affordable. The Simms Freestone Wading Boot is another great option to consider. These Simms products are recommended by many professionals.

Compass 360 Deadfall STFT Breathable Waders

As the name implies, they are breathable waders and they are quite affordable. They are made of strong fabric, last long, and are comfortable. They give you your money's worth.

Chapter 4: Selecting the Main Components: Rod, Reel, Line, Tippet and Leader–Putting It All Together

In this chapter, we are going to learn about the three main considerations when selecting a fly rod. We will also learn how the reel pairs with the fly rod. Finally, questions will be answered about what type of line, tippet, and leader complete the fly rod.

If you wish to purchase the rod and reel separately, the key to finding the right reel is dependent upon the weight, length, and action of the rod. The second option, most likely the best for beginners, is to have a salesperson or guide advise you which reel and rod combination to purchase. Buying a reel separately is somewhat difficult due to the large variety of reels available and the factors that need to be considered. There are a lot of things to take into consideration before buying a fly reel, so having good background information about them is a step in the right direction. Fly reels can be grouped into two based on their drag system. The purpose of the drag is to provide resistance when reeling in a fish in order to control the retrieval. The two fly reel groups are; the disc and the click and pawl. We'll learn about these later on in this section.

The Fundamentals of Fly Fishing

The fundamental premise and difference between fly fishing and spin fishing is that the line itself is weighted whereas in spinning the lure acts as the weight. The line is then worked up and out of the rod by repeated casting in order to precisely place the artificial lure onto the water. Usually, fly rods have pre-determined weights, or thicknesses, with similar line weights for getting the best results. The standard fly rod weighs around 5-weight (5wt). Flies are imitations of insects in one of the various stages of their lives. They vary by season, locale, and elevation, just as real insects do. However, the basic insect types generally imitated are the Stonefly, Mayfly, True fly, and Caddis flies. A fly reel should be sized to match the rod and line you intend to use. Midsize fly reels are commonly used for 4-6 weight rods. If you are able, try to select a large arbor reel with a larger circumference, so as not to crimp your fly line when it is spooled.

Choosing a Fly Fishing Rod

Fly rods are created to direct a fly onto the water. Momentum is used to control the direction and distance for the placement of the lure. The rod should be chosen based on the size and strength of the kind of fish that you intend to catch as they are instrumental in being able to land your fish. Modern fly rods come in varying lengths, weights and flexibilities. Fly rods are sized by weight, which is determined by the size of the fly line that the designer thinks is the best for the rod in question. A 10-weight rod is built to cast a 10-weight line, and a 15-weight rod is most effective when paired with a 15-weight line. The stiffness of the fly rod is matched to the varying line weights.

The difference between rod sizes becomes increasingly larger as the size gets bigger because variations in line weights also become proportionately larger. What differentiates a 5- and the 6-weight line is not the same as what differentiates a 13- and 14-weight. So all other things being equal, the heavier the fly line, the more sturdy a rod has to be for it to cast well. Nonetheless, it should be kept in mind that even within the same category, different rods can have varying "actions" or flex profiles. "Action" as used in reference to a rod is a word that has been used to refer to the ability to flex in a particular area, stiffness, and speed of "recovery" which refers to the swiftness with which the movement at the end of the cast ceases. In any particular rod size, certain rods may be very stiff in the "butt" area and have malleable tips. On the other hand, some kinds will be bendable in the middle section of the rod. Others are designed to be more rigid along the entire length.

Many designers of fly rods have done away with the subjective term "action". Instead, when they talk about a rod's performance characteristics, they are referring to the ability of the rod to flex in different areas. They may refer to a rod as having a "progressive taper", or "stiff butt". "fast tip", "tip flex", "soft tip", or "mid flex". All of these terms are not very useful in themselves until a deeper look is taken at why rods are manufactured with different performance goals. If a rod is built properly, chances are that it will load properly with the line in question. If a rod is being utilized for casting a matching line and a fly is connected to it, it should be as effective at 10 feet as at 60 feet. However, a stiff rod will only be effective when cast at longer distances.

It may also be that a rod that performs well at close distances is typically softer. This is due to the fact that softer rods make it possible for the caster to feel the loading of the rod at a faster pace, with only a little line out of the rod tip. Meanwhile, long casts can benefit from having more line out of the rod tip because there is more weight to throw. A stiff rod, on the other hand, makes holding more line in the air easier. It casts well for short distances and for longer distances. We say this type of rod has the right "load" characteristics as far as the line in question is concerned. The designer of a rod can then personalize the manner in which the rod is crafted by choosing the part of the rod they intend to bend more or less. Manipulating the rod to arch around its tip, mid, or butt section can be utilized to go on to define the rod for the caster. This may be for the purpose of matching separate casting styles or matching the requirements of a particular fishing situation. Now that you get the picture of how things are done, we will analyze the two ends of the spectrum.

Firstly, you are searching for a rod that you will use for catching reasonably sized fish as well as smaller trout. The flies that you will be using will be less weighty and not very large, usually sizes 12 to 20. So the intention for your rod is to be able to cast it over short distances. For this reason, you may not find it necessary to cast beyond 30 feet. The best fit to use in this kind of fishing are rods that flex well from its midsection to its butt section. This is often called the "traditional" or "slow" action rod. A rod that flexes in the middle section may also be a great fit for this kind of fishing. Meanwhile, you do not necessarily need a stiff butt section to be able to fight the fish. Nonetheless, it is very important that you have a rod that you are able to "feel" when you get the leader out of the rod tip.

Also, you want the rod to be able to "feel" the momentum in the line once you get it out to 15 to 30 feet. As a result, 2-, 3-, and 4- weight rods are the best for this kind of activity. In another context, let's say you intend to carry a rod for bonefishing. These types of fish are stronger and faster. They can weigh up to 10 pounds and move at speeds of 30 miles per hour. You also have to keep in mind that you will be battling environmental forces such as the wind when you are casting. The lures needed for your outdoor sporting activity come in a lot of sizes. This means a rod with a butt section that is stiff enough to trap these fish as swiftly as possible. It also needs to have a flex profile which is mostly flexible from its tip to its midsection. These kinds of rods increasingly flex toward the middle section as more line is cast out. The rod that you will be using should preferably be tipped toward the extreme side of the "load range". This helps you to cast more effectively with 20 to 30 feet of line extending from the tip of the rod rather than the more common "slow" rod can.

When you encounter these types of circumstances, an 8- or 9-weight rod is a great option. Complete rod tapers and flex profiles are novel ideas in fly fishing. Before PVC fly lines were invented, there were few differences in fly lines and as such, there was little need to design rods with special performance characteristics. Over the last fifty years, this type of outdoor sport has incorporated a greater range of species in different fishing environments. Whereas fly rods can generally be grouped into one-handed or double-handed fly rods (double-handed fly rods had initially been created in Scotland as a means of covering an expansive body of water) the different modes of manufacturing and customizing fly rods for particular fish, fishing techniques and conditions are a lot to list. This makes selecting a fly rod something of a challenge since there are small incremental differences in performance characteristics but also because each fly rod designer will tout their product as the best on the market..

This section will provide step-by-step tips to guide you in determining which fly rod is the best fit for you. Before anything else, you need to decide the size by choosing what species of fish you are after. When fishing for trout, yet want a versatile rod for catching trout up to 20 inches, a 5-weight is a great option for consideration. However, if you want a rod specially designed for catching small fish in high-altitude streams, a 3- or 4-weight is a better option. On the other hand, if you are seeking to catch salmon and other larger fish, anything smaller than a 7-weight may well be lacking. An 8-weight rod for bonefish would be great for saltwater fly fishing. A 10-weight rod would also be a good choice for barracuda and small tarpon. For larger tarpon, a 12-weight rod would be suitable. The bigger the fish, the more attention should be paid to the size and usefulness of the rod as a fly fishing tool. Typically the most prevalent sizes of one-handed rods go from 7 feet to 10 feet. The 9-foot rod is a great length which provides versatility in fly fishing. Other alternatives are considered for a rod that is not so long for fishing on brushy creeks or longer rods that are designed for a particular purpose, for example, certain types of nymph fishing.

The next consideration is to decide on the rod construction material; rods manufactured with carbon graphite fiber or others manufactured from traditional cane, also referred to as split bamboo. Some fly fishermen fancy customized designs and a more classic style so they would go preferably for bamboo rods. These types of fly fishing rods are usually less affordable than their high-tech equivalents. The higher cost is mostly due to the skill required in crafting them as opposed to the materials used in the process. Thirdly, you need to ponder over whether a 3- or 4-piece rod is needed to be attached to a backpack or carried on a plane. Alternatively, find out if a 2-piece rod that might likely be left strung up for a lengthy period of time is easier to use. When you have chosen the preferred size, linear measurement, and fabrication, as well as the sum total of pieces, consider the cost. Many companies keep cost in mind and you will be able to find an affordable option whether you want to be conservative or go the custom, top-quality route.

If you are a novice angler, it is improbable that you will cast a rod that costs more than $500 differently than one which costs less than $200. However, it is worth noting that fly casting professionals will gravitate toward a rod that is in the less expensive region of a fly rod manufacturer's price list. After you have made up your mind about the price that you intend to pay, you have to consider the offers from different designers. Fly fishers usually gravitate toward a particular brand of fishing rod due to the characteristics that manufacturers build into their equipment. When you've done your research about the manufacturers that design the fishing rods that you want, at a cost that seems right to you, start selecting among the different brands in the fly shop. Beginners should opt for a fishing rod that they are comfortable with and that increases their desire to continue casting. As you gain mastery through consistent practice you can determine with precision if a particular rod is suited for your level of performance and casting techniques. In the end, the decision you make will be a combination of factors including the cost, and the characteristics built in by the designers. Relying on an expert at the store to help in selecting the best combination would be good to consider as a novice.

Matching the Fly Line and Fly Rod

Choosing the right gear is necessary for success in any sporting activity, and the same is true for fly fishing. Being new to angling, selecting the right tools can seem daunting. However, once you have a rod and reel picked out, you will need to choose the type of fly line. There are different fly fishing lines for novices but some of the excellent choices are where the intent of matching the casting technique and fly presentation make the most sense. This is on account of the differences between fishing lines and casting. The ideal fly fishing line is important and necessary for a great fishing trip. In our modern world, there are a lot of brands of fishing lines on the market that are particularly designed for very specific target audiences. The distance cast, line mass, and prevailing weather conditions can determine the effectiveness of the fishing line. Some are useful in all water conditions, whether sinking or floating. There are designs for catching stronger and larger fish. Take a keen look at the fly rod in your possession. Fly lines which are ideal for a specific rod are not the same particularly because of different rod action. Keep in mind that a fast action rod will load more easily and be less difficult to cast with a heavier line and an aggressive front taper. In the same vein, a moderate action fly rod is most effective if it is joined to a lighter fly line with a longer taper. In this next section, we will be looking at some of the excellent fishing lines to start with.

Piscifun Fly Fishing Forward Weight Floating Line
This is one of the more popular products on the entire fly fishing market for many novices. On inspection, you will realize that these fishing lines are diligently manufactured and have many color options. What distinguishes it from other products is the superior design and tough composition. Their lines are braided, making them strong and sturdy equipment in the angler's toolbox especially when working against larger fish or conditions like rocky bottoms or submerged branches that could abrade the line.

KastKing Exergy Fishing Line
If you are just starting out as a fly fisher, this fishing line is one of the best options for you. It is one of the most reasonably priced on the market, with several benefits. Many anglers consider it one of the most popular fly fishing lines available since it performs effectively and gives you great fly fishing methods.

Orvis Clearwater WF Fishing Line

When starting out, Orvis Clearwater WF Fishing Line is a remarkable option to consider. It has been designed with novices in mind. It is worth knowing that this fishing line is manufactured in the United States and is one of the best on the market. Because of its quality, you can get the best results out of it. The line is very thin and light. Moreover, it comes with a unique external layer, for reducing its friction against the line rail.

SF Braided Fly Line Backing

This fly fishing line is a great choice for those who are just starting because of its price and simplicity. This fly fishing line is made primarily of polyester or dacron. The material increases rigidity around its central point and it is resistant to UV rays and resistant to decay. Because of this, there is virtually no chance of it breaking apart in saltwater. You get good value for your money. It is also one of the best options when it comes to catching large fish weighing between 45 to 70 pounds.

All About the Fly Fishing Leader and Tippet

By now you may have come across the names leader and tippet. This section addresses the questions and concerns about the fly fishing leaders and tippet materials.

Fly Fishing Leader and Tippet–the Basics

Besides the essential tools needed for angling; fly rods, reels, lines, and artificial flies, you need to learn how to connect the line and the fly before you cast them into the water. This is where the leader and tippet come into play. The leader and tippet almost seamlessly connect the fly line and the flies. There are many different types of fly fishing leaders and tippets on the market. One major purpose of fly fishing leaders and tippets is for linking the fly lines to the flies using materials that will not frighten the fish when they land on the water surface. Another use of leaders and tippets are for completing the transfer of the momentum created in the fly lines into the casting stroke. After moving it along the line and down to the fly, the line rolls over and arranges itself into a straight line. If you cast your fly and land somewhere unintended, you will not be very successful in enticing the fish to take your fly. But before anything else, let's discuss what a leader and tippet are.

Definition of Fly Fishing Leader and Tippet

You need to be able to distinguish a fly fishing leader from a tippet. Simply put, leaders are the length of line connected to the butt end of fly lines (the end furthest away from the caster). They are thicker and heavier where they connect to the fly line but reduce in weight and thickness as they taper toward the end where the tippet is connected. The leader will look like the fishing monofilament used on the spinning or casting reel. The part of the fly fishing leader which is attached to the fly line at the butt usually has a higher pound test rating. Many fly fishers prefer a 20-pound test at the butt end connected to the fly line and reduce it to maybe a 4-pound test or so. This leader will usually be about 9 feet long. This is fine when you are just starting and understanding the fundamentals of angling. Leader materials in fly shops are usually labeled as 4X, 5X, etc. The 'X 'rating as used in fly fishing will be explained in further sections.

Tippet is a specific gauge monofilament line that is attached to the end of the leader, to which you tie the fly. The tippet is usually the smallest gauge line on your rig and is virtually invisible to the fish. Tippet is also very flexible and allows your fly to float or swim more naturally. Using the lightest, yet sturdiest possible tippet without the fish noticing it is the aim here. The tippet size is based on the kind of fishing and the general conditions. Now that we understand the dynamic between the leader and the setup, we need to dive further into the subject to increase your understanding.

The Setup of the Fly Fishing Leader and Tippet
We have already established that the weightier leader material is connected to the fly line's butt section. Lengthwise, it is advisable to start with 9-10 feet as a novice angler. The length may be reduced or extended depending on the given situation. As far as a leader setup is concerned, you aim to build a taper from the butt end down to the thinnest part of the tippet. It makes it easy for energy to move from the leader and tippet in order to make it lie straight. You may want to begin with a 20-pound test leader material connected to the fly line and reduce it, which warrants the remaining length of your material to be connected to your tippet. This provides the best ability to fool the fish you are chasing without it perceiving the line that is attached to the fly. Reducing a 20-pound test to as low as a 6- or 4-pound test is often a difficult task in just 9 feet. Handcrafting custom tapered leaders is a vast topic. You can browse the internet and find a lot of varied articles for custom tapers and the reasons for designing them. Our advice is to look into the many pre-made knotless tapered leaders in local fly shops. They are fairly new inventions where angling is concerned since you receive the best taper with no knots to trap weeds or debris found in aquatic habitats. Find a tapered leader without knots within the range of 7 to 9 feet that reduces to 3X or 4X (the 'X 'rating will be explained soon).

The Materials Used to Build a Fly Fishing Leader and Tippet
The fly fishing leader and tippet are made up of two main types of materials. These are fluorocarbon and monofilament. Each is best used when matched to the kind of fishing intended. There are some differences between a monofilament and fluorocarbon. Monofilament is generally stretchier than fluorocarbon. It moves much easier on the water. Fluorocarbon, on the other hand, is not as elastic hence it is very sensitive and its hooksets are strong. It cannot float on water for long, it's more durable and is abrasion resistant because it is solid and made of stronger material. Fluorocarbon is also almost invisible to the fish. Nonetheless, fluorocarbon is more likely to have its knots broken than

monofilament. It also requires proper lubrication when the knots are cinched down. Also, fluorocarbon is costlier than monofilament. However, they are both useful when fly fishing. Because it is expensive, many people do not want to try fluorocarbon. But it is undeniable that both of them are great assets when you are out on the water. So you need to make up your mind about the type of fishing you will be engaging in. With fluorocarbon sinking faster and providing higher abrasion resistance and greater sensitivity, it is a good option when nymph and streamer fishing. But because monofilament floats well, it is a good option when fishing dry flies.

The 'X' Rating System of the Fly Fishing Leader and Tippet

The 'X 'rating system used in the context of the leader and tippet does not have to confuse you. The designers adopt a system of rating which is marked by the letter 'X'. This simply denotes how strong the fly fishing leader and tippet material are as well as their diameter. The rating system ranges from 03X and is reduced to 8X, with 03X excelling in thickness and strength and 8X being less thick and slighter. To put it simply, the 'X 'size designates its strength and thickness.

What Pound Test is 4X?

4X is virtually the same as a 6lb test. The X system for leaders and tippets is a novel concept for a lot of people. 5X would equal about 4lb while 3X would equal about 8lb. The pound test usually vacillates among various designers, however, they are usually near the same range.

Practical Application

If you are considering the 'X 'size tippet to connect your fly to, a basic principle for determining this is taking the size of the fly and dividing it by 3. If, for example, your fly is 16, dividing it by 3 would give you 5.3333. When approximated, you would get a 5X tippet size. If the fly in your possession is a size 4 streamer, 4 divided by 3 would give you 1.333. When approximated, it is a size 1X tippet. It is a basic principle for finding the right tippet to use when fly fishing.

Fly Fishing Leader Size Guidelines

The division by 3 is not a perfect fit for all kinds of situations. It is just a system that guides you to get the best tippet size. Sometimes, the final choice depends on what feels right to you as well as the prevailing conditions. Ask yourself if the fish are larger in the water where you are fishing. Another good question to ask is if there are more snags you could catch onto if nymphing. Is the trout, for example, very alert and easily frightened when it is around the tippet or should you opt for something that is more akin to nature which allows the fly to move with ease and not be hindered by the leader and tippet? All these are necessary for discovering the tippet size that you will be using. At the end of the day, the final decision boils down to several variables depending on the dominant conditions. There are certain instances where the division by 3 principle does not even work for you, so you will have to let it go and find other alternatives. The circumstances that you are fishing in may dictate a different line of action and you might have to decide your tippet size based on other conditions. So let it be an estimation for guiding you and find out if it is possible to make do with the larger tippet size. A little trial and error may do the trick, if you do not attract some fish, reduce the tippet size and find out if there are any improvements. You will know the kind of size fly to use when you continue to practice. There are no steadfast rules to follow, just tips to guide you as you go. You will find that in many instances, the techniques that you use will either work or won't work. However, the mistakes allow you to learn and they eventually make you wiser. But make sure you have all the fun in the world while you are at it. Fly fishing is a sport that requires you to keep learning. It will continue to challenge you till you become a master, but you can never truly be perfect at it. You have to put yourself out there and try to see what works for you in the situation in which you are fishing that day. Fly fishing leader and tippet do not need to be complicated when you are learning the basics of fly fishing. By now, you should have a fundamental knowledge about the leader and tippet, their uses, and why they are necessary tools.

What Length Must the Leader Be for Fly Fishing?
A lot of dynamics come into play for determining leader length, some of which are the type of fishing you are engaging in as well as the situation at hand, but the typical length is around 6-12 feet long. A 9-foot tapered leader is a great choice to begin with. If you are seeking to catch spookier fish, you can stretch it out to about 12 feet. If you are fishing for wilder species, making use of a 6 to 7.5-foot tapered leader is a good choice. A leader which is not as long is effective when you fish for streamers because it allows you to guide the weightier flies.

Some of the Best Fishing Knots Every Angler Should Learn to Tie

Whether you are a novice or master, you can increase your success while fishing by learning the styles of knotting shown here. Knowing how to tie knots is a basic skill every fly fisherman must learn. As with entomology, casting, and fly tying, you can use the Keep It Simple, Stupid! (KISS) principle or you can take the time to become proficient in an important subdiscipline. While tying a Bimini twist or a Duncan loop is not as interesting as fooling a big brown fish, it is an essential part of the wonderful world of fly fishing. Fly fishing fascinates many because of its myriad intertwined areas, and how deeply you can engross yourself in each area. You do not have to begin with complicated knots. You can multiply your success as a fly fisher with the styles of knotting listed in this section. The tippet, backing, fly, fly line, and leader are simply a progressive system, however, if you purchase a package that has been assembled beforehand, the individual parts have to be linked together with a knot. You need to know the knots that will be used for adding a tippet and tying on a fly at the end of the line and you will have to do this many times during each fishing trip. Several basic knots, however, can be learned easily. You are not an ineffective angler if you have to go back to a reference for tying up a lesser-used knot, say an arbor knot occasionally when a new reel is acquired and you intend to add backing. It can also be interesting to tie new knots. You will realize that certain knots are difficult to tie whereas others are less difficult, and you might even learn new tricks for tying knots. So many systems are available for connecting the various parts of your fly line system. You will find some trusted and time-tested methods in this section and the reasons behind them.

Backing

The first technique we will begin with is backing, because that is one of the earlier things you will need to deal with when starting with an empty reel. The backing supports you if you catch a large fish which uses up most or all of your fly line which may extend to even 100 feet. This is not a usual occurrence during fishing, however, it is likely to occur when you are on a large, rushing body of water, and you are using small flies or light tippets. In the event that you encounter such a problem, you need backing for filling up the extra space in your reel, because it is made to hold a fly line in addition to some amount of backing. Whether or not you intend to catch a large fish, there is the need to fill the reel arbor with an appropriate amount of backing. If not, your fly line will become coiled tightly around the narrow spindle which makes it harder to operate. With certain reels, there are indications in the innermost parts of the spool frame to show the extent of filling these reels with backing. Alternatively, you can fill about one-third of it or till it becomes half full. It is a good plan to purchase your fly line and backing at a specialty fly shop. It is not necessarily due to the fact that the workers have useful tips to offer regarding quality lines that are customized to your needs but based on the fact that they have a line winder that spools line onto your reel quickly and in the best way possible. Some outfits will provide this service at no charge. Looping backing on a reel requires that you invest your resources, one of which includes time (150 yards at one inch per crank). The winding must be done correctly around the reel arbor. When loose coils of backing are wound at the base of the arbor, those at the top must be tightened. This could be when you catch a large fish, or simply when the backing is wound around the reel. After that, the coils which have now been tightened get buried beneath the loosened coils, thereby producing a snarling sound which is likely to jam your reel. The backing should be wound around the reel in the correct manner to prevent inconveniences. You are responsible for putting the backing on your reel if you do not hire anyone to perform the service for you so take time to do it properly. A more effective line of action may be to wind your backing when your reel is attached to your rod, so connect your empty reel to a rod in the position you want to crank. If you cast using the right hand, you will feel the need to crank counterclockwise with the free hand. Because of this, you ought to lock your reel to its seat with its handle tipped leftward. Hold the farthest part of the backing across the spool while threading it through the rod. After, pass the thread in and out of the reel line guard. Do the same to the spool arbor. Finally, remove the thread out of the line guard. Such a technique is useful if you have attached the backing to a spool using the arbor knot. Winding the backing requires that there is a friend or anyone nearby to run a pen through the backing spool and hold both to the far tips of the pen to allow the free movement of the spool. When winding the spool around the reel, move its backing over the pages of a telephone directory to produce an effect of tension. Or run the backing over wrapped towels. When that is done, you can place your foot over the towel to produce the tension you need for winding the backing so there are no loose ends. When cranking the reel for the purpose of winding the backing, move the backing back and forth across the span of the spool to allow it to wind evenly and not accumulate at just a certain part of the spool (Fly Fisherman, 2020). Once your reel is a third or half full of backing, fasten a double surgeon's loop at the end of the Dacron backing. Ensure that the loop is not too small to allow the passage of the line spool through it. Follow these steps to make a double surgeon's loop. First, double the line to create a loop that is large enough so that the reel can pass through it. In addition, extend it by some inches while holding both lines together. Further, create a simple overhand knot and make sure that you keep both lines at the same moment. After, pass the loop through the overhand knot three more times. Finally, tighten by pulling on the loop and the standing line. Pull on the tag and trim. (Fly Fishing, 2020)

Fly Line

A lot of modern day fly lines are manufactured with welded loops at both ends. It costs more to purchase a line with powerful loops for catching even the most stubborn fish. You can make an equally powerful loop for your fly line that is not manufactured with any. To connect the loop of backing to the loop in your fly line, pass the large backing loop through the small loop in the fly line end and then pass the whole fly line spool through the backing loop to create a loop-to-loop connection (Fly Fishing, 2020). You ought to ensure that the loop-to-loop connection is seated correctly. Your loops must resemble square knots. If not, the connection might become too big and may not pass through the rod guides with relative ease. To make a whipped loop, you need to follow these steps. First, slice the end of the fly line at a 45-degree angle with a razor blade for a smooth transition. Further, pull approximately 12 inches of thread through the bobbin. Remove the thread spool and make five turns of thread around one leg of the bobbin to increase tension. Once the thread is securely attached, spin the bobbin by moving both your hands in a forward motion, wrapping the thread between your two hands. Guiding the thread with your hands, slowly work down the transition area. After the loop is secure, start swinging the bobbin around the doubled line, making enough wraps to cover the 1 inch of doubled line and the tapered end. To tie a whip-finish knot, place a loop of monofilament along the thread wraps. Make a dozen more wraps over the monofilament. After, pass the thread through the monofilament loop. Finally, pull the thread under the wraps, forming the whip-finish knot. Coat the wraps with Pliobond. You cannot use the loop-to-loop method with thin, gel-spun polyethylene backing, as under pressure it will cut through the welded loop of the fly line (Fly Fishing, 2020). Dacron backing is one of the best recommendations for a novice angler. It is less expensive and easy to use.

Leader

After completing the tasks mentioned above, you need to attach the tip of your fly line to the leader. The tapered monofilament which connects the tippet and fly is between 7 to 12 feet long. Fly lines and tapered leaders without knots come with loops which allows them to be joined together. The loop of the fly leader is passed through the far end of the fly line. After that, the leader's tip is then passed through its loop. It is necessary that your loop is seated properly in order to create square knots with them. You do not need to fret if your line does not come with loops because there are several other methods of connecting it to the leader. Some of these methods are creating a loop at the tip of the line or using a nail knot to create a perpetual connection. It is worth noting that no one uses a nail to tie a nail knot. Meanwhile, a plastic tube that is similar to a part of a ballpoint pen can also be used. Because of the wide variety of nail knot tools available, it makes the process simpler. Follow these steps to make a nail knot. First, put the fly line tip just beyond the tube. Place the farthest part of your leader above your line. Then, wrap the line and tube with the leader. After, continue wrapping toward the tip of the fly line until you have a total of six wraps. While holding the wraps tightly, put the butt section of the leader inside the tube and shove it. Gently remove the tube while continuing to pinch the coils. After, take the leader and pull its ends to make sure it is tight. Snip the tag end of the leader as well as the excess fly line. Coat the knot with flexible cement (Fly Fishing, 2020).

Tippet

Unlike the leader, which is tapered, the tippet has a uniform diameter and should be the same diameter or slightly thinner than the terminal end of your leader (Fly Fishing, 2020). Mono means one so a monofilament has one filament, and it is manufactured with either fluorocarbon material or nylon. Nylon monofilament is usually limper than fluorocarbon, and this makes it easier to get it seated and allows for the flies to more easily drift on the water. Fluorocarbon is inelastic and can withstand corrosion. It is also more expensive. It is also not easily seen in the water. A lot of fly fishers love these lines because they are difficult to detect and more likely to fool fish into taking the bait.

Anytime the fly is changed, the monofilament reduces in length. Your leader tapers down, so tying flies directly to the leaders is not an advisable line of action. Also, a level-diameter tippet section, especially a fine, thin 4X, 5X, or 6X tippet, is extremely limp and does not turn over and land straight like your leader (Fly Fishing, 2020). It, therefore, adds slack into your system and makes it more likely that you will be able to fool fish. Two pieces of monofilament can be connected by a blood knot and the surgeon's knot (Fly Fishing, 2020). You do not have to learn the two different methods of knotting because each of them does the same thing. However, the surgeon's knot is preferred by a lot of people because they believe tying it is less difficult. This section will guide you in making a surgeon's knot. Both lines which will be used must have their ends across from each other. Proceed by tying an overhand knot, keeping the two lines together. After, pass the two lines through again for a surgeon's knot. Pass the two lines through one more time for increased security with lighter tippets. Finally, tighten by pulling on all four strands. The finished knot should resemble a figure 8. To make a blood knot; first, both lines which will be used must have their ends across from each other. Take the working end of the first line five times around the other line. The active end must then be passed through the two lines. Pinch with the thumb and forefinger to maintain this gap. The active end of the second line must be wrapped around the first one five times. Insert the tag of the second line in the gap opposite the tag of the first line. Both lines ought to enter the gap through different paths or else the knot will fail. Place the two tag ends between your teeth, lubricating the wraps at the same time, and slowly pull the standing lines in opposite directions. Finally, trim the tag ends and test the knot.

Fly

The knot which is the most important knot in many people's estimation because it occurs at often the weakest part of the system is the tippet-to-fly connection (Fly Fishing, 2020).

Usually, many people attach the improved clinch knot to the fly. Tying it is not very difficult and it has a track record of catching fish, however, many professionals will not advise you to go for it because it is not as strong as other types of knots.

The Pitzen knot, however, is very strong and one of the most dependable ones out there. It is also known as the 16/20 knot, the Eugene bend knot, or simply the fisherman's knot. Follow this guide to learn to tie a Eugene bend knot. Before anything else, pass the tippet through the eye of the hook and form a 6-inch open loop. The loop should be wrapped against the standing line thrice. When this is done, the end of the tags should be passed through the loop. Then, pull the tag end away from the hook to dress the knot and lubricate it (Fly Fishing, 2020). The line's standing end should be pulled at till it gets to a point where the knots can glide across it to the fly. The knot pops when it is seated correctly. Finally, clip the tag. It is possible to learn about the strength of this knot when you simply tie two hooks together using one thread of nylon monofilament. Attach the Eugene bend knot to a hook and an improved clinch knot on another one. Drive a hook into a board while pulling the other hook using a tool such as a plier. Regardless of the one that is initially pulled, the breakage always starts with the improved clinch knot. Breaking strength is not the only thing to consider when you plan to tie a knot. If you are using a 6X tippet, you want the knot to be as strong as possible because you have no margin for error, but if you are using a 15-pound-test fluorocarbon, a weaker knot is still pretty strong (Fly Fishing, 2020). When it comes to heavy tippets you ought to consider the movement of the flies in the water, and when using a clinch type knot whose tippet is heavier, the flies are rigid in the water. When this happens, consider using the no-slip loop knot. Saltwater guides and permit guides were some of its well-known users. Today, a lot of people use it since the most important requirement is a weighty tippet. It is effective because it is attached to the tippet in a flexible manner. It has liberty to slide across the monofilament. This knot is especially useful for catching trout.

The No-slip loop knot. First, you need to tie a simple overhand knot in the line before passing the tag end across the hook's eye. After, move the tag in and out of the overhand knot in an even rhythm. Pulling the tag in a gentle fashion till the overhand knot is close to the hook's eye. Make five turns around the standing line, working away from the hook. Your tag should then be passed through your very first overhand knot. Finally, pull at the fly, the tag, and the standing line all at once to make it tighter.

Fly Fishing Reels

Many factors must be taken into consideration when purchasing a new fly reel, so it pays to understand the distinction between how they are made and what their different features are for coming to a satisfying choice. Fly reels can be grouped into two based on their drag system. The "drag" causes friction inside the reel that creates resistance to slow the fish's ability to run with your line. It is controlled using either the disc or click and pawl, both with different ways of working. We will start by breaking things down below.

Disc Drag

Reels which have a disc drag are similar in function to brakes in cars. You tighten or loosen discs against the spool of your reel so that it does not move quickly. This invention is still beneficial to anglers in the modern world. Some of the components of the disc are corks, which require frequent lubrication to function properly. It also needs to be prevented from coming into contact with sand, silt, and other debris that are often encountered on the water.

However, if you are not big on a tool that requires continuous maintenance, but has features that are almost as easy to adjust, then go for one that has a sealed drag. They work very well both in freshwater and saltwater. Many USA-based brands are building high quality sealed disc drag reels. Hatch, Nautilus, Galvan, Tibor, and Ross are just a few of the solid brands available today. They have different features and specifications depending on what species you plan to target and where you want to fish. Sealed drags are a great tool to have in the saltwater setting because their internal components are often built from polymers that do not require the reapplication of lubricant. Slightly rinsing them after use is enough to keep this tool sturdy for a very long time. Always remember that salt is highly corrosive, so you will want to ensure to get rid of any trace of it from your line and your backing as well as your reel. Waterworks-Lamson, which has not been mentioned till now, is a manufacturer in Idaho. They provide a distinct sealed drag system that is conical and easily adjustable by turning its knob.

With traditional disc drag reels, it is essential to make the drag loose when you are done using it or before storing it. It is done for the safety of the discs. Where Lamson's conical drag is concerned, the surface area of the discs is made into a pair of cones which require deftness to machine. They are relatively affordable which is part of the reasons why customers love them. The biggest takeaway for disc drag reels is that they can stop larger fish and that the ones with sealed drags are most useful for saltwater fishing.

Cast Versus Machined

In the previous section, we mentioned that the affordable reels provided by Lamson are cast aluminum. We will be looking at its implication in this section. When casting, you pour melted aluminum into a mold. This allows faster production than machining but also creates a harder product. Harder is not a bad thing, however, it can make it more brittle, making it more prone to cracking or breaking. You should keep this in mind if you are especially clumsy. Machined aluminum is molded from a bigger block or billet into its final desired shape through a controlled material removal process. This process leads to a final product that is lighter weight and slightly more durable. It is also easier to repair, but more importantly, it gives you a more desirable surface for anodizing. Anodizing makes the surface of the aluminum last longer and prevents corrosion. In simple terms, the metal is kept safe from harsh weather conditions. If you are looking for a well-priced reel that still has a great drag and is resistant to weather and environmental factors, then go for the cast options. However, although the machined reel is pricier, you get your money's worth.

Click and Pawl

The click and pawl are more old-fashioned. This type is better suited for smaller stream fishing. Its design is not complicated and a lot of unnecessary components do not exist between you and the fish, which many anglers appreciate. Disc drag reels oftentimes come with a mechanism that clicks to indicate how fast the fish is taking out line. The click mechanism was invented as a result of the OG click pawl reels, where adjustment of the drag is nearly impossible, so the angler presses their palm against the spool to stall the movement of fish. It can be quite hard to become competent in this skill and the chances of losing fish are higher in this scenario when you are initially getting a feel for it. You may even end up with some bloody knuckles from your reel handle. The loud clicks that are produced when a big fish claims your lure are wonderful and hard to beat. Hardy, a manufacturer in England, makes some of the most popular click pawl reels in the fly fishing world. These reels have a strong following, and while some people keep them as relics and not for fishing purposes, other people use them for fly fishing and keep them properly maintained. Hardy has been around since 1872. One important thing to make a mental note about click pawl reels is that their internal mechanism is completely exposed. It has one or more pawls that tick against the gear's teeth. The absence of a seal makes them very unsuitable for saltwater fishing. The small, exposed parts, like the brass components, do not take well to exposure to harsh elements. That is why it is necessary to give the utmost care to these reels. Keep them clean and well lubricated to lessen the chances of corrosion, even from just silt and freshwater. Some reel designers have a lot of pawls for increased drag resistance. However, these reels have an adjustable drag for engaging or disengaging the pawls against the gear to make its resistance less or more. A machined aluminum reel with a 6-pawl drag, meant for steelhead fishing, can be found with a simple google search. The biggest takeaway for click and pawl reels is that although they are classic, noisy, and a lot of fun, they do require some maintenance because of their construction. You will find a ton of history about them and they are amazing for freshwater fishing, particularly small streams and swing fishing.

Center Pin

Also, we have center pin reels. If you look at a center pin reel, you might think that it is a fly reel, and that is the only reason they are being incorporated in this section. Center pin reels are designed for casting terminal weight and are more like a spinning or bait fishing reel. They hold monofilament rather than fly line. They are also used primarily for fishing with floats, jigs, bait, or other lures. More interestingly, they do not come with drags, which has the benefit of making drift fishing more effective since the line is allowed to release spool when casting is taking place. If you use center pin reels, you can introduce a whole new thrilling element into your fishing, but mastering the art of casting them is quite difficult and may take some time.

Notwithstanding the kind of reel you pick for the rod setup, the last piece you will need to make up your mind about is the drag direction. A lot of reels come with the drag position to the left-hand retrieve. This is the most common form for those who cast with their right hand. If you are left-handed or a big game saltwater angler, you will likely want the drag to be right-handed. This can often be done at home yourself, but some reel manufacturers such as Nautilus do not have an interchangeable drag and that is something you should look into before purchasing. If you are buying a reel that is preloaded with a line or backing, pay attention to the direction too. Switching a lot of drags is not very difficult, yet if the line is on, removing it and respooling it is required to avoid line tangling.

Chapter 5: A Place to Start–Types of Flies

Dry and Wet

Dry fly fishing does require a bit of practice on the water and serious dedication to master. Dry fly fishing is an interesting form of fly fishing. Casting a fly on the water and patiently waiting for the fish to take the bait is sort of an addictive experience. During dry fly fishing, the fly does not sink in the water. Initially, this technique was used to fish only for trout. Meanwhile, there are several other methods that can be used to catch trout. Trout have been observed to feed at the bottom of the water. They swim toward the surface when a flying or terrestrial insect attracts their attention. Being armed with this knowledge, anglers use dry flies as bait for trout. Sometimes, salmon can also be caught using this technique. Dry fly fishing attempts to imitate the movement of a real fly on top of the water. To catch a large number of fish, you need to study the type of fish you intend to catch and their environment.

The techniques used in dry fly fishing vary with regard to the type of fish you intend to catch. Many people engage in this sport in the mornings as well as the night because flies usually hatch around these times which attract the fish. Anglers can trick fish using the artificial lure during these peak periods.

What Are Flies

Flies are made typically to mimic real insects or other types of fish food. Today, they can be found on the market in different varieties. When they are cast the right way, the flies fall into the water so they are visibly available to fish. Tying flies yourself is not child's play and may require consistent practice to master. As already mentioned, the two main categories are dry flies and wet flies, but there are also others such as nymphs and streamers. Learning about both dry flies and wet flies and finding out which are suited for different conditions will make you more effective as an angler.

Wet Flies Versus Dry Flies
The lures used to fool fish into believing that it's real food come in many different designs, all of which are supposed to be an imitation of real insects. You need to do the preliminary task of studying everything about the environment you will be fishing in to pick the right

fly for fishing there. A lot of flies used to fish are either wet flies or dry flies. Our job in this section is to learn and understand all there is to know about wet flies and dry flies.

Angling Technique

Lines and floating files are necessary for success in fly fishing. These are connected with a leader which is not easily seen where the fly is knotted, and a small part of it is replaced with nylon. A lot of the fish's food is moved by the current, so the fish usually look upstream in an attempt to get their food. The angler, therefore, must keep this fact at the back of their minds. Some fish, including trout, have good vision, so the angler has to be tactful in his operation. They attempt to catch their food where the slow-moving and fast-moving waters meet. Another thing the angler ought to know is that large rocks in the water are a good resting place for fish while waiting for their food. The fisher must then stealthily present the fly to the fish so that he does not spook them or alert them of his presence. In the end, the angler's aim is to fool the fish into believing that the bait is a real fly. If it is done correctly, the fly will move naturally so that the presence of the fly line is not perceived. While all these things are taking place, the angler must never lose focus. Because of the instability in the movement of the water currents, it is possible that the drift of the fly can be disturbed. Mending refers to the lifting and movement of the part of the line that needs to be re-aligned with the direction in which the fly drifts. The movement of the current which carries the fly determines the position of the mend. You have to ensure that mending the fly line does not obstruct the way in which the fly line will move normally. Mending is easier if the fly is visible. Dry fly fishing requires that you engage your all and the thrill that comes with catching a fish is worth the effort expended. It can be addictive. However, if you catch a fish, it may moisten the fly, making it more likely to sink. Cast a fly backward and forward to get it to dry quickly. A piece of moisture-wicking fabric can also be used. A dry fly that can no longer float can be substituted with a fly that looks almost the same while the other fly dries. When it completely dries up, apply a water-repellent to it. To cast a dry fly, you will need to possess a level of skill. Because the tippet and leader you will be making use of may be lightweight, the probability of tangling up the fly is higher. That is why you need to exercise patience when using your casts and let them completely unfurl before you make your next move. Using shorter casts is a great way to master casting fly rods. Anglers find themselves in trouble when they are trying to make a 35-foot cast with a size 22 dry fly. Stay close and pick the spots near you where the fish are feeding.

Dry Flies

The way a dry fly is manufactured allows it to fall gently on top of the water without absorbing it. It does not have to be necessarily light. Oil or water-repellent is usually applied to them. A dry fly is thought of as a freshwater fly. Dry flies are either imitation or attractor types. Imitations mimic adult insects, both the ones on land and in water. A lot of imitators can be built for different types of insects. The Royal Wulff attractor is a great option for novices since it is clearly visible. Another imitation such as a parachute Adams is a great option because its landing is gentle, quite like real flies on the surface of the water and it is also very easy to see. Visibility is an added advantage for the novice. The difference between an artificial fly and a real fly should be scant to increase your chances of attracting fish. Imitation flies, for example, are great options to consider. Some other great options are salmon flies, like Parks' salmon flies, although they are much bigger than trout flies. It is more difficult to fish with dry flies as compared to wet flies, and for those who are just starting, the process of mastering the correct casting methods can be tougher. If you fish with wet flies, it takes some time for the fish to notice them after they land on the surface of the water. When the landing of the fly in the water is too obvious or disturbing, the fish are unlikely to be scared off by the disturbance created because they are far from the surface. However, you cannot afford this carelessness if you are using dry flies because the types of fish you intend to catch are not deeper in the water. Although dry fly fishing entails a lot, the thrill attached to it is higher when compared to wet fly fishing, because you are able to see everything as it takes place on the surface. Dry flies can mimic different foods in an attempt to fool fish to come to the surface. Some of these foods are the adult insects which we have already mentioned much earlier in this chapter. Dry flies can also pose as other choice fish food such as mice and frogs. Depending on what type of fish you're targeting, there is always going to be a dry fly that will entice them to eat. Both wet and dry flies vary in form and design, although anglers prefer certain types over others. Dry flies are not very large and their wings are quite fluffy.

Fly Fishing Dry Flies in a River

Engaging in this exercise is exciting. You need to closely observe the ripples created on top of the water. Some of the ripples may be caused by flies, yet the biggest ones will usually be fishes looking out for flies on top of the water. The flies you choose will largely be based on the movement of the current. After you choose, cast toward it and allow the fly to move downstream. If the fly is convincing enough, a fish will take the bait almost immediately. You will be less likely to catch fish if none takes the bait just moments after it lands on the water. Allow your fly to finish its natural drift and prepare yourself for another round of casting. However, you must not allow your fly to stay in the water for an extended period of time.

Dry Fly Materials

Dry flies have narrower bodies and the materials used for building them are lighter. Some of these materials include thread, feathers, and fur. Chemical flotant is often used to treat the fly to enable them to remain on top of the water.

Fly Selection

The benefit you get from tying flies is the ease of matching aquatic foods in the water. Before they are taken to the tying bench, these aquatic foods ought to be grouped. After, match them with the best patterns listed in this book. Ensure that the correct colors are used to customize the flies. Keep a keen eye out for the nitty-gritty of your fly. Ensure that your tied fly mimics the details of what seems natural. Doing this will increase the likelihood of your success because you may be able to catch a larger quantity of fish. The color of the aquatic food depends on the water habitat. If these foods match their surroundings, the better. Meaning they ought to look like the weeds and the rocks in the environment. Feel free to incorporate creativity in the process of tying. The process of selecting food that fish might like may lead to a greater catch. It is these small things that distinguish a great fisherman from a mediocre one. Fish do not stint themselves when it comes to what they eat and an angler has the responsibility to know these types of foods and ensure that their lures are a good imitation of them. The website provides a list of insects that can be found on land and these include ants, grasshoppers, mice, moths, lizards, earthworms, beetles, and crickets (Love the Outdoors, 2022). The same website also mentions insects that can be found on the water and some of them are caddisflies, mayflies, stoneflies, midges, crane flies, dragonflies, damselflies, crustaceans, forage fish, leeches, and eels (Love the Outdoors, 2022). You can either observe the eating habits of fish or study these using the internet or resources in your library. Start by watching the surface of the water for insect activity. Carrying a pair of compact binoculars will help a great deal in your analysis. You can capture a specimen such as an insect using an aquarium net. Do this by placing your net just beneath the surface of the water where you observe the fish. Again, this net can also be used to catch flying insects. Studying a spider's web for insects trapped inside can help you determine the types of insects available in that particular environment.

What Is A Wet Fly?

Wet flies are man-made imitations of insects that are manufactured to lure fish under the water. Usually, wet flies are designed with a heavy part to help them sink easily in the water. The name of this part is a "bead head". Its weight pulls the fly under the water. When fishing deep, or fast water, it is often necessary to utilize a fly with weight or to fish with added weight on your line to present your flies at the proper depth.

On the other hand, using wet flies without beads may be more effective for water that is not too deep because beads may scare the fish or cause the flies to sink quicker than is necessary. Wet flies can be made to look like a number of fish foods. Sometimes, wet flies are built to sink to the deepest parts of the water, whereas others are built to reach just below the surface. Wet flies are preferred by many beginners because they are easy to use. Sometimes, fishing in deeper waters does not entail much skill and expertise because the fish below are not easily frightened by sudden movements. Getting the hang of casting can be challenging, and the best of the best also make mistakes sometimes as far as this technique is concerned, so wet flies are something of a blessing in this regard because any foul-up on your side is less likely to scare the fish. Observation has taught us that fish feed at lower depths much of the time rather than on the surface of the water. So, if fish are hardly showing up on top of the water, if you are serious about catching any, you would need to make use of wet flies. Some expert anglers usually fall on wet flies because it requires using less effort on the water and you may even catch more fish. Even fish that usually come to the surface to feed find the better part of their food in the dark depths, therefore, making use of wet flies makes it more likely that fish will be drawn to the flies.

Wet Fly Materials
Wet flies need to resemble what the fish would usually eat, so a variety of materials and structures are used for imitating insects during the various stages of their life cycle. Nymphs are usually beneath the depths, while emergers are struggling to come out of the water to continue their life cycle.

What Are The Differences Between Wet Flies And Streamers?
Streamers are an example of wet flies which are manufactured to resemble larger fish. They are among some of the biggest fly fishing lures and can sink far beneath the water as well as flow alongside the current to lure fishes. Streamers are built in a manner such that their eyes are prominently placed for visibility. They are used almost the same way as wet flies, although they are much heavier. The wooly bugger streamers are a well-known type of streamer.

The Commonest Types of Wet Flies
Wet flies are well-known among anglers and are very different in their design. Typically, they come with wings, bland colors, bead heads, as well as streaming tails. They come in different colors and sizes. DesMarais mentions some common types of wet flies including Prince Nymph, Zebra Midge, RS2, Wooly Bugger, WD-40, San Juan Worm, Pheasant Tail Nymph, and Copper John (DesMarais, 2022).

Fly Fishing Hook Sizes
A lot of the flies used to fish come with hooks between the sizes 12-20, a 20 is typically small and very fragile. Due to the length of dry fly hooks, it can be difficult to tie them. Nonetheless, keep in mind that it is possible to find bigger dry flies. Some patterns, for instance, are bigger because the prey that they are trying to imitate are bigger. If you are just starting out and are attempting to understand flies, you can get confused while reading about the sizes available, particularly when it becomes necessary to select the correct size to fish with. To select the proper size, you need to get an idea of what the fish

feed on. In certain instances, it is more sensible to use smaller flies to trick the fish, whereas in other situations, using bigger flies is a great line of action. The key takeaway here is to let your flies mimic the usual diet of the fish.

The Differences and Similarities Between Dry Flies and Wet Flies

Always keep in mind that dry flies remain dry and wet flies remain wet. Both are used in very different contexts but sometimes they can be combined.

Single Wet Fly

A typical wet fly rig comes with several components to alert you of the position or location of the fish as well as other key things that make fishing effective. Single wet fly rigs are the best options for novices and they do not get tangled easily. As you progress, you can use other types.

Double Wet Fly

Double wet fly rigs have a bottom fly followed by a fly that resembles it or anything that is around the top of the water. Double rigs improve the probability of increasing your catch on a single drift, which accounts for their popularity among anglers. But keep in mind that the more flies, the higher the chances of them getting tangled up. Therefore, novices should only use them when casting in locations that do not require more advanced skill and deftness.

Single Dry Fly

A single dry fly rig has one fly tied at the end of the line. It is very popular among anglers because of its simplicity and some also tie two flies at the end in a bid to attract fish.

Dry Dropper Rigs

With these types of rigs, dry flies are combined with wet flies. Wet flies are attached to the end of the line and dry flies are placed just a little above them. When immersed in water, the wet fly is quite similar to when it is attached to a single wet fly rig and the same goes for the dry fly when placed on a dry fly rig. These types of rigs serve many purposes and they can be used to catch fish in all settings. Therefore, it is prized highly by a lot of anglers.

Wet Fly Fishing Techniques

Using wet flies to fish may not be as much fun, however, you may be able to increase your catch using them. There are several techniques used by anglers when fishing with wet flies and they are; Dead drifting below an indicator, Swinging streamers across the river at about a 45-degree angle, Stripping streamers through the water downstream, or in still water, Euro, Czech, or tight line nymphing without an indicator, Sight fishing with wet flies (simply trying to spot the take), Downstream nymphing/swinging.

Dry Fly Fishing Techniques

Unlike wet fly fishing, many anglers find dry fly fishing thrilling, although you are not guaranteed a bountiful catch. Some of the things anglers need to pay attention to during dry fly fishing are:

● Casting from an appropriate position to get a proper drift

● Mending to get a proper drift

● Utilizing the right fly and matching the hatch

Selecting the Right Fly

At this point, the reader should have a basic understanding of wet and dry flies, their distinctions and similarities as well as their uses. Anglers should go outdoors with a variety of flies to experiment with and try to match the conditions of the day. Some of the things to keep in mind in selecting the right fly will be discussed below.

Key Considerations

The Water

You need to consider the characteristics of the water you will be fishing in such as its depth, the speed of its current, the nature of its bottom, and areas where fish usually feed, among many other things. All these factors will help you determine the best fly to use for such a situation.

Bugs

There are many things to consider here, such as whether or not the bugs are hatching. This helps you to determine whether or not your flies should mimic any of these.

Can You Spot Fish Feeding?

If the fish are visible from where you are standing, are they feeding or not? Where is their position? The key here is to realize that seeing the fish is an advantage you should use to learn all that you can.

Season & Water Temperature

This is important to find out whether or not the bugs are hatching, the level of the water, the position of the fish, and their feeding habits. The knowledge of the season and how it affects the warmth and coldness of the water can help in determining the correct flies to choose for fishing.

Using Dry Flies to Fish in a Small Stream

Fly fishing in small streams is the most demanding and will require you to use all your fly fishing skills. It entails mastery and accuracy in casting. The fish you will be trying to catch are easily frightened so any wrong move on your part and they will move farther away from you. However, there are fewer places for these fish to hide and they are very selective about their food so you need to use the right fly and be tactful about how you present them to the fish.

History

Dry fly fishing became very popular in the nineteenth century, when Frederic M. Halford published the books *Floating Flies and How to Dress Them* as well as *Dry Fly Fishing in Theory and Practice*. He designed false flies to resemble real ones yet this was not always the case. It compelled J. W. Dunne to propose a theory about trout vision from which came the idea of using imitators designed to be used in hotter atmospheric conditions. The book was released for public consumption in 1924 under the name *Sunshine and the Dry Fly*. Around the same time, G. E. M. Skues started a form of campaign about wet nymph fishing. He promoted and supported the use of attractors which were made to goad fish rather than trick them. The conservatives preferred using the dry fly and were not very happy about Skues 'promotions so, in 1938, the opposition of the Flyfishers' Club eventually culminated in a prejudiced investigation against this young man. Nonetheless, Skues' approach was very helpful to a lot of anglers during that time.

Fly fishing can be traced back to ancient Rome where red threads were used to fool fish. In addition, the Japanese practice of Tenkara was one of the earliest forms of angling. Weighted lines were used then but not reels. Around the late fifteenth century, *A Treatyse of Fysshynge wyth an Angle*, written by Juliana Berners, is considered to be the first book on fly fishing released. The first fly fishing clubs were formed in Britain around the nineteenth century and many books on the subject were released. Back in the United States, fly fishing garnered a lot more attention and interest around the late nineteenth century when several people started fishing for trout in rivers. The invention of the fiberglass rod and the synthetic line also helped to popularize the sport. Today, many people across different age ranges participate in the sport. Aside from books, there are also movies about fly fishing, a popular one being *A River Runs Through It*.

Chapter 6: Casting–Do Not Be Intimidated

This chapter will destroy all those mental barriers about the difficulty associated with casting and ensure more efficacy as you continue to practice.

Fundamentals of Casting a Fly Fishing Rod

To cast a fly rod, you need to throw the reel to the line so that it unrolls and goes out in front of you (Chavez, 2022). To be effective at casting, your wrists ought to be soft and your whole body has to be engaged in the process for smooth rotation. Contrary to popular belief, there are a lot of methods for casting fly rods. Every angler gets accustomed to a certain technique of casting based on their experience on the water.

Fundamentals of Using a Casting Rod

You need to understand the basics of casting a fly rod before you can be effective at it. A very obvious one is that a false fly is used and not a real insect. These man-made flies have bushy wings and lots of furs, which you tie to the end of your line.

This section focuses on casting the fly rod properly. The necessary tools ought to be available before you proceed to cast anything. Pliers are one such necessary tool for freeing tangled items. The fluorocarbon leader is important in such situations because it reduces the likelihood of tangling. The necessary equipment are fly rods, fly lines, leaders, backing on the reels, and a quality fishing fly. If you have these, then you can proceed to cast.

How to Cast a Fly Fishing Rod

Fly fishing is a fun sport but entails a level of difficulty. Like everything in life, mastery at casting a fly rod takes time, yet the basics can be understood by anyone. First, adjust the line to rig it correctly in order to make a good cast. After, start practicing how to use the overhead cast. If you get the hang of the fundamentals, use a roll cast to approach fish stealthily in unusual spots.

Putting the Fly Rod Together

First, you need to put together the segments of the fly rod. The rod must be removed from the case holding it. Before anything else, focus on the two pieces beneath the rod, because of their size. Slide both pieces together and begin twisting them as lightly as possible so that both dots on its side can be aligned. The pieces that are left must be slid inside the rod and both dots on each section must be lined up. Forcing the rod segment can break them. Your segment starts thinning out around your rod. After that, your reel must be slid inside the reel's seat around the base of the rod. Your reel seat holds your reel firmly and is located at the base of your rod. Your reel must be connected to your rod when the bottom of your reel is slid in the open spot at the highest point of the reel seat. The nut near the base of your reel seat must be twisted in order to make it tighter around your reel. Twitch your reel in order to ensure that you have safely connected it. Then, a loop knot should be created around the extreme part of your fly line. The far part of your fly line must be connected to your leader, which is the slim line that attaches a much thicker fly line to your tippet and fly lure, and its tippet, which cannot easily be seen by fishes and is used for holding the fly lure firmly. This is for stringing the lure. Make for a lot of slack in your fly line and create a loop knot around its farthest section to make it easier to connect the leader and even switch it at a future date. You have to ensure that you spool your fly line around the reel so it is tight. Use your fishing knot to attach your leader to the farthest section of your fly line. The leader ensures movement along your fly line which is thicker on the rod to the much thinner tippet. This leader is thicker around its end which is attached to your line and reduces into a small line that is connected to your tippet. A fishing knot is then tied to join your leader to the thick end of your fly line. In addition, your leader controls the movement of your line on the water. Your leader ought to be around nine feet long to adequately separate your fly line from your fly lure. A number of leaders come with metal clasps that may be attached to your fly line's loop.

Also, a tippet should be attached to the farthest part of your leader and you achieve this when you tie it using a knot. Tippets are thin lines attached to the ends of leaders and flies. It cannot easily be seen by fish in the water which makes it difficult for them to discern that anything is attached to your fly. Your tippet should be attached to the farthest part of your leader and a fly is then connected to the tippet's end. Using nail knots helps to secure the connection between your tippet and your leader. The tippet should be a minimum of 4 feet long. After, attach a fly lure to the end of the tippet with a sturdy knot. The flies have hooks attached to them for trapping fish that try to eat them. Your tippet should then be passed into the eye of your hook and attach a fly to the farthest part of your tippet using a fishing knot. Make your line moist to increase its flexibility to make it possible to tighten the knot that is tied. You need to pull the tippet and the leader to make them straight and ensure that they are safe to use. The fly line should exceed the length by 1-2 feet. The fly line's heaviness is responsible for effective casting, therefore, the weightier line needs to be pulled out and this should precede casting. A simple strategy for ensuring that you do not run out of fly lines is to get to your reel at the base of your rod with, say, 1 to 2 feet additional length.

Assembling the Fly Line
Before anything else, you need to connect your fly line to your rod by attaching a loop to its end. Gripping the fly line firmly in a hand, pull a loop of line from under it through the

guide using your free hand. Release the loops to get a long length of loose line in the middle of both hands. Pass it inside the rod rings. Then place your finger on top of the end of your fly line in order to create a loop, and guide the remaining line through it. The finger should be withdrawn from the bottom of your loop. When you are done with this, ensure that it is tightened around the fly rod's handle.

Casting Overhead

For performing this cast, the fly rod should be held over your head. Hold it firmly. Reach out your index finger and place it over the line. The remaining length of the line should be held down with your free fingers. Further, lower your hand till it reaches your waist as fluidly as possible. This should be done swiftly to reduce the chances of the loops entangling themselves. Also, you need to utilize your overhead cast to accustom yourself to casting a fly fishing rod. To master the overhead cast, you need to have knowledge of loading the rod correctly, and loading in this sense means working to find the tension in your lines and poles to make for casting your fly lure. So it is incumbent on the novice angler to understand the fundamentals of using the overhead cast. Performing the overhead cast is more difficult in the face of obstacles such as lowered branches since your line may become entangled. Also, it is required that you are standing with your feet separated by a shoulder width. When casting within a short range, you need to use a parallel stance to make for stability in your body posture and to increase the likelihood that you will "feel" the heaviness of the fly line on your rod. The distance between your feet ought to be even and your weight should be at your center and not on your heels. When casting at long distances, it might be easier for you to stand with a foot propped forward to allow you to reach at your rear for a stronger cast and not trip and fall. The rod should be held with your thumb above the grip. Your press should be minimal else the likelihood of performing the quick stop nearing the end of the stroke will be hindered. Your squeeze should be light and your rod should be held in line with the target area you want. Let your rod lie inside your fingers and the grip should only be tightened when it is compelled to stop at the end of each stroke. Consequently, the end of your fly rod must be kept linear to your forearm. Ensure your rod's reel is tipped toward the floor. Also, lay the line right before you on the floor. To create just the right amount of momentum in your backswing, stretch up to 10 feet of your line at the farthest part of your rod. Your line should be aimed in a straight pattern while you stand squarely facing this target. Your leader and tippet, however, must not become entangled. Equally important is the action of bringing the rod upward and back in one swift movement. The tip of the rod should be kept lowered till you are prepared for casting and using in one swift, fluid movement to drag the rod upward and behind you.

It will in turn lead to bending in some parts of the rod and build tension in others. When you snap a long whip, for instance, its line moves upward and it trails behind you in a huge arc. Further, stop the rod abruptly once it passes a vertical position. If the rod above your head is straightened and passed away from you, you should stall its movement so its line remains behind you. The rod should be held motionless when the line is traveling behind you. Consider stalling the rod when it gets to the 1 or 2 o'clock position at your back. Furthermore, let your line unroll freely in the space at your back. Even as the rod remains stretched at your back, bide your time for the moment when the line travels at your back and rises to the point when it is being unrolled. The energy created as a result of the movement behind you will create a sort of motion till it reaches the point when it is fully extended. You need to patiently leave the line to unroll completely. If your line tapers down before it fully unfurls at your back, there is no need to invest too much effort into your cast. The line should be straightened before you and the process repeated. In addition, your rod should be moved forward so that your line is brought before you. When the line is completely unfurled in the space at your back, stroke it smoothly to propel your rod forward. Eventually, your line snaps forward and a loop is created in the air because of its movement. Straighten your wrists and ensure that your elbows are touching your body so that you can move smoothly. Then, the tip of your rod should be lowered as your line unfurls before you. Your rod should be stopped when it is almost equidistant with the floor so that the line's energy moves it ahead. During the process of unfurling, drop the tip of your rod gently so your line rolls out to your fly at the farthest section. Your line ought to end at the point you intended for it to. The rod should not be snapped down aggressively because the tension created in the line due to this may result in your cast dropping further down even before it gets to the fish.

Performing a Roll Cast

Performing the roll cast involves holding your fly rod in one hand and using the other to hold and release loops of loose lines. Your arms ought to reach your waist after which they are swung forward in an arch far from the water. This makes it possible to make a full turn when you finish casting. The tip of your rod should be lowered when doing this. The steps ought to be done repeatedly till you get to the required distance for fishing. Your wrists should be kept supple while you cast. The necessity of doing this is greatest when performing overhead casts because the consequences of inaccuracy are dire. Keep your wrists flexible while casting to reduce the likelihood of sustaining injuries.

It is important to remember that the roll cast is done when angling is being performed around narrow waterways. The roll cast causes your line to unfurl over the water with ease and reduces the chances of spooking the fish, however, performing it is a bit demanding. It is equally necessary that your line is dipped in water due to the fact that the water anchors it as well as gives you the chance to form a loop. Roll casts are useful tools especially when you are fishing in streams. They are also essential in the event of a typically annoying wind behind you that is preventing you from effectively performing an overhead cast. Next, your rod should be drawn upward and backward for the purpose of dragging your line's end across the water. Starting out by using maybe 25 feet of the line extended before you and pointing the tip of your rod over the water is an advisable line of action. The movement should be done slowly so that your rod can be brought back and your line should be dragged on top of the water. However, ensure that your line is not pulled out of the water. The friction created as a result of your line coming in contact with the water makes it easy for you to cast your rod. The stroke is stopped when your rod is tipped high if a loop was created at your back. When the rod moves beyond a vertical position, maintain that stance. Your line has to become droopy at the back of your rod's tip at this point, and a loop is formed in the process. A bigger loop generates more energy which makes casting more effective. When the loop is created by moving it back, your rod should be propelled forward to begin casting forward. Raise your hands and your rod should point up. Your line begins rolling over the water's surface and follows the movement of your cast. Your movement should be controlled at this point. Finally, casting should be ended by ceasing movement so that your line unfurls. The loop rises when the rod is moved forward. The cast should be stopped when it is almost parallel with the water. Your loop then rolls out over the surface of the water and its movement will be determined at that point based on the direction of your cast. Let the end of your line fall over the water lightly.

Casting With Different Types of Rods

The rods used for fly fishing include parabolic rods, double hauling rods, and single-handed rods.

Parabolic Rods

Parabolic fly rods are ideal choices for novice anglers since they can be used with relative ease by almost anyone and the fundamental rudiments of using them for casting can be understood quickly. The shortfall of using parabolic rods, however, is that their accuracy is not as powerful as the other types of rods. Controlling your line is not as effective with this type of rod as compared to the other types. The manner in which these rods are used can be likened to the method of performing an overhead cast. You need to hold them at the level of your waist and your arms should move like circles away from your body in order to complete a rotation.

Double Hauling Rods

These rods allow you to cast the farthest. More power is developed from these casts by building extra momentum with each throw. Using the Forward Spey casting method is essential when you get to the proper distance. It allows the line to unfurl before it hits the point you are aiming at without getting tangled up.

Single-Handed Fly Rods

These rods are essential for catching fish that are just a little below the water's surface, and they do not tangle up easily. The Forward Spey cast method is useful if you intend to adopt this fly rod. Also, it is necessary to use a hand for holding them at the level of your waist and keep your arms swaying far from your body. Always keep it at the back of your mind that your wrists must remain supple as you do this. When you do it the right way, you will get a perfect loop that can be easily mended by trimming the unwanted line that is in the way while still maintaining its quality.

Various Forms of Casting-Review

Back Cast

It is a fundamental casting technique where you have to bring your rod back behind you while holding the line with your other hand. Proceed by sending it further ahead so that it is far from you and at the point where you intend to cast till your arms are straightened before you.

The Forward Cast

The Forward Casts include the Forward Spey and Forward T Spey. A Forward Spey is ideal for those who are just starting out since it is not necessary to haul twice while you are at it. What is required is just to extend your fly rod using both hands at the level of your waist and proceeding to throw them ahead when you use momentum built by swaying both arms. Unlike Forward Spey, Forward T Spey requires extra effort since you have to follow one additional step. Performing this cast requires using the arm above the line to tug it down till it becomes rigid before sending your rod behind you to perform a different Forward Reach while holding it firmly. Always remind yourself never to change hands till you prepare yourself for a backlash.

Forward Reach

These are easy to do and can be performed in different bodies of water. The key requirement is maintaining your hold on the line with a hand and tugging it gently at the same time till your rod is above your shoulder and its tip is pointed up. You can do this while you stand, sit, or crouch and this makes it ideal for catching fish that usually come to the surface of the water. Your rod should be moved from behind you with a powerful backward sway of your arms till it unfurls before you.

Forward T Reach

When doing this, you only need an arm since the other one grabs your line firmly rather than constantly tugging at it. A number of double hauls are also required for Forward T Reach. This technique involves bringing the fly toward yourself and a loop is left for a spectacular cast.

Forward T Cast

Forward T Cast can almost be compared to Forward Reach. The only difference is that you need to perform double hauling before you start. Because of this singular reason, Forward T Cast may not be as easy to master yet you have the opportunity to get rid of unnecessary slack that might get entangled if not discarded swiftly. Performing Forward T Cast requires that the rod is brought behind you with zero movements of your arm across the line before releasing it with a hand and using the second one to pull down the line to make it rigid. After, it should be brought before you quickly at the point you intend for your fly to fall.

Forward Cast

Knowledge about a Forward Cast is a necessary requirement if you intend to fish or practice casting. It entails your rod being held out before you with a hand and moving a wrist at its extreme side to allow the line to be thrown as straight as possible.

Roll Cast

People do not usually use Roll Casts, however, it is needed for making Forward and Forward T Casts less difficult because they double the length of the cast. Performing a Roll Cast involves holding your rod before you with a hand. At the same time, you need to roll your wrist up two times before it is jerked forward at the end.

Various Techniques

Rod Tip High

In the process of performing this cast, the tip of your rod should be extended skyward and your right hand should also be moved up at the same time. Throw out your arm to your targeted area as swiftly as possible. This ensures that a lot of momentum is built behind every throw when they land on the desired points. This reduces the tangling which occurs with the line and fly.

Rod Tip Pointed

If you intend to use a Forward or Double Hauling Cast, the tip of the rod ought to be pointed in the direction you aim at before movement begins. This allows it to fly in a straight line and reduces the likelihood of it getting tangled up in the process. It also prevents slack which usually occurs as a result of improper throws from forming between your line and fly. Keep your arm loose but ensure that it is sturdy enough for throwing your line up while performing this cast. Also, keep your wrist supple during the process. To avoid injuring yourself or reducing the quality of your casts, do not jerk forward.

The Correct Way of Holding The Casting Rod

Line Completely Straight

To perform Forward or Forward T casts, your line needs to be straight. It should be kept this way throughout the process to avoid the formation of slack which is not wanted.

Parallel Stance

To perform Forward or Forward T casts, the rod should be held between your hands as you maintain a parallel stance. Be careful and keep an eye out for unnecessary movements in the process of performing this cast since the chances of tangling up the fly and reel are higher when you do this.

Conclusion

What Is Fly Fishing?

Fly fishing is considered one of the finest forms of angling (fishing), primarily due to the beautiful motion of fly casting, as evidenced in the movie *A River Runs Through It*. The sport is a fishing technique that uses a setup that differentiates from fishing in that you use a "pole" in lieu of a fishing rod, the line is weighted and the casting is done in a continuous manner in lieu of casting and then leaving the rod until the fish bite. The idea is to trick the fish into believing that the fly is an actual insect so that they will "bite" the bait.

Mental Benefits of Fly Fishing

- Fly Fishing is an avenue for relaxation; the sound of rushing water soothing the mind and the concentration of placing the fly exactly where it is intended to go.
- Fly Fishing Reduces Stress. In the war against stress in our lives, fly fishing offers one of the most promising positive effects of being in the great outdoors.
- Fly Fishing Provides a Cure for Depression. The flowing water and fresh air can have an almost instantaneous effect on your mood and prevent feelings of anxiety, fatigue, and depression.
- Fly Fishing Provides an Avenue for Networking. Our human nature requires that we interact and form connections with other people. Fly fishing makes this possible.
- Fly Fishing Boosts Your Brain Power. The fresh air from the outdoors can have major advantages for your short-term memory.
- Fly Fishing Gives You Perspective. It ignites your creative powers, which prepares you to find strategic ways to cope with the challenges that come with life.
- Fly Fishing Boosts Your Self-Esteem. When you eventually master the skill of casting and catching fish on your fly rod, you get an improved sense of self-worth.
- Fly Fishing Increases Feelings of Happiness and Excitement. Fly fishing also prevents feelings of tiredness and depression by leveling your melatonin levels. It also allows you to take a break from your normal activities and unwind accordingly.
- Fly Fishing Is Therapeutic. It also offers proximity to nature, and the chance to catch fish either for food or just for fun. But more than this, fly fishing improves the individual's mental state.
- Fly Fishing Improves Focus and Patience. Time spent in the outdoors is appreciated by both your body and mind because it provides a disconnect from technology and those other things that are constantly placing a demand on your time. Fly fishing has a calming and meditative effect on your brain. This helps to boost your concentration.

- Letting Go And Non-Attachment. You can decide to pay attention to your breath as you hold the fly rod, calming your mind and body.

Physical Benefits of Fly Fishing

- Fly Fishing Lowers Your Cortisol Level. Anglers are also less likely to exhibit Post Traumatic Stress Disorder (PTSD) symptoms and experience low levels of depression and anxiety.
- Fly Fishing Offers a Full Body Workout. Fly fishing is for people of all ages. So seniors looking to engage in less intense forms of workout can consider fly fishing. The exercises are less demanding as compared to those done in the gym and you get to choose the extent of your movement on the fishing trip.
- Fly Fishing Has Healing Properties.

The Nine Best Locations For Fly Fishing In The United States

- California. This location is home to the Yuba River, the Sacramento River, the Yosemite National Park, and the Owens River, all of which are great places for fly fishing.
- Montana. Montana is home to Rock Creek, which contains a wide variety of fishes.
- West Virginia. The New River, Gorge National River, and Bluestone National Scenic River are other great locations for fly fishing in West Virginia.
- Alaska. The Nushagak River and Togiak River are just a few in this State.
- Colorado. Colorado is home to the infamous Colorado River as well as the Blue River.
- Florida. The Florida Keys, for instance, is rich in various species of fish including tarpon and bonefish.
- Wyoming. The Snake River which boasts some of the largest fishes is found in Wyoming
- North Carolina. This State hosts a stretch of water that is home to different species of fish, especially trout.
- Pennsylvania. Some of the most well-known limestone streams, springs, and creeks are found in Pennsylvania.

Some Elements All Good Fishing Vests Must Possess

- Pockets. The ideal fly fishing vest must have a number of pockets that come in different sizes. These vests need to be big enough to store a lot of fly boxes.
- Velcro. Pockets sealed with Velcro are very easy to open and are almost as safe as actual pockets. In addition, Velcro is very durable.
- Quality zips. A good zip is needed for the safekeeping of accessories that are too valuable to lose.
- Clips and attachment points. People hate temporary fixture points and would rather opt for the permanent ones which can increase their chances of securing a

lanyard. This is to prevent them from losing simple tools such as line clips and forceps.
- Quick drying. Anglers love a fishing vest that can dry within a short space of time. A vest that does not dry quickly makes a good environment for mold growth. It also increases the odds that the metallic equipment stored within it would corrode quickly.
- Color. Many anglers want fishing vests that match their surroundings.

Recommendations for the Six Best Fly Fishing Vests
- Simms Freestone Fishing Vest.
- Patagonia Mesh Master II Vest.
- Columbia Men's Henry's Fork V Vest.
- Gihuo Men's Fishing Vest.
- Astral Ronny Life Jacket PFD.

Choosing the Correct Pair of Fishing Waders
- Hip Waders. These are very comfortable and cost less when compared to the other wading systems which will be mentioned in this section.
- Chest High Waders. Although they cost an arm and a leg, these are very versatile products which are very popular in the fly fishing market.
- Waist-High Waders. These are typically waterproof pants that do not exceed the length of the waist. It is the choice option for several anglers during hot seasons.

Clothing to Wear Under Waders Based on the Season
- Winter and Very Cold Weather. Warmth is essential, especially during the winter. A jacket can be a great top layer. Additionally, a vest can be worn to increase your bodily warmth. Hoodies can be added to these because the hood can act as a windbreak which you might need.
- Spring, Summer, and Fall. It is not important to wear layers of clothing during the summer. The weather conditions do not allow it. However, you must put on the appropriate clothing to maintain the proper body temperature when you are on the water. T-shirts, jeans, work pants, and wader pants are some of the appropriate options to consider. However, wearing shorts on the water is not advisable.

This book provides you with everything you need to become a proficient angler. Now that you are armed with this information, go into the outdoors and become all that you can be.

References

Carrick E. (2021). *The Best Places To Go Fly Fishing In The U.S.* Travel and Leisure. https://www.travelandleisure.com/trip-ideas/the-best-fly-fishing

Chavez D. (2022). *How To Cast A Fly Fishing Rod: The Basic Techniques for Success.* Fishing Outcast. https://fishingoutcast.com/how-to-cast-a-fly-fishing-rod/

Credihealth Team. (n.d.). *Are There Health Benefits of Fly Fishing?* https://www.credihealth.com/blog/are-there-health-benefits-with-fly-fishing/

DesMarais M. (n.d.). *Wet Flies vs. Dry Flies: Everything You Need to Know.* Hiking and Fishing. https://hikingandfishing.com/wet-flies-vs-dry-flies/

Edwards S. (2015). *Fly-Fishing and the Brain.* Harvard Medical School. https://hms.harvard.edu/news-events/publications-archive/brain/fly-fishing-brain

Fly Fisherman. (2020). *8 Best Fly Fishing Knots You Should Know How to Tie.* https://www.flyfisherman.com/editorial/9-best-fly-fishing-knots-you-should-know/368780

Hanson D. (2020). *7 Psychological Benefits of Fishing With a Fly Rod.* Take Me Fishing. https://www.takemefishing.org/blog/october-2020/7-psychological-benefits-of-fishing-with-a-fly-rod/#:~:text=The%20focused%20attention%20and%20rapid,to%20cope%20with%20life's%20demands.

James R. (n.d.). *5 Health Benefits of Fly Fishing That Might Surprise You.* Fly Rods. https://flyrods.com/5-health-benefits-of-fly-fishing-that-might-surprise-you/

Kepka B. (n.d.). *The Health Benefits of Fly Fishing.* Fly Fisher Pro. https://flyfisherpro.com/blog/fishing-and-mental-health/

Lepage J. (n.d.). *Choosing a Fly Fishing Rod.* MidCurrent. https://midcurrent.com/gear/choosing-a-fly-fishing-rod/

Losee C. (2020). *Fly Fishing Leader and Tippet: What, Why, and How.* The Fly Fishing Basics. https://theflyfishingbasics.com/fly-fishing-leader-and-tippet-what-why-how/

Matechak E. (n.d.). *What to Wear Under Waders (Fly Fishing, Cold, Warm, etc.).* Freshwater Fishing Advice. https://freshwaterfishingadvice.com/what-wear-under-waders/#:~:text=%20Wading%20leggings%20can%20be%20a%20great%20piece,more%20comfortable%20to%20wear%20than%20jeans%20or%20pants

MaxCatch. (2020). *What is the best fly fishing line for beginners?* https://www.maxcatchfishing.com/faq/what-is-the-best-fly-fishing-line-for-beginners.html

Mooers D. (2020). *Dry Fly Fishing: An Angler s Guide.* Into Fly Fishing. https://intoflyfishing.com/dry-fly-fishing/

Reynold M. (2022). *How to Cast a Fly Fishing Rod.* WikiHow. https://www.wikihow.com/Cast-a-Fly-Fishing-Rod

Robinson C. (n.d.). *Choosing the Correct Pair of Fishing Waders.* Bcfishn. https://www.bcfishn.com/fishing-waders/

Schoenberger L. (n.d.). *What is Fly Fishing: A Beginner s Guide.* The Wading List. https://www.thewadinglist.com/what-is-fly-fishing/

Trout Resource. (2021). *The 6 Best Fly Fishing Vests and the Reasons Why.* https://www.troutresource.com/2021/08/06/best-fly-fishing-vest/

Wikipedia. (2022). *Dry fly fishing.* https://en.wikipedia.org/wiki/Dry_fly_fishing

William. (n.d.). *The Best Rivers To Fly Fish In California.* Fly Fish For Fun. http://flyfishforfun.com/best-rivers-fly-fish-california/

Women's Fly Fishing. (2021). *1700 or so Words about Fly Reels.* https://womensflyfishing.com/blogs/women-on-the-fly/1700-or-so-words-about-fly-reels